YOU'LL BE SCARED.

Sure–you'll be scared.

– Fear, Stress, and Coping in the Civil War–

by

Philip M. Cole

Best wishes,
Philip M. Cole

Colecraft Industries
Since 1981

Colecraft Industries
970 Mt. Carmel Road
Orrtanna, PA 17353

e-mail: colecraftbooks@embarqmail.com

website: colecraftbooks.com

ISBN 978-0-9777125-9-5

PRINTED AND BOUND IN THE UNITED STATES OF AMERICA

First edition

Cover design by Philip M. Cole

Contents

Source Key to Illustrations
[Note: captions to illustrations may not be from original]

A. Berghaus = ABG	James F. Queen = JFQ
Albert Bierstadt = AB	Allen C. Redwood = ACR
J. Becker = JB	W. L. Sheppard = WLS
C. E. H. Bonwill = CEHB	W. Taber = WT
Currier & Ives – C&I	J. E. Taylor = JET
Edwin Forbes = EF	James Walker = JW
C. E. F. Hillen = CEFH	Alfred Waud = AW
Winslow Homer = WH	William Waud = WW
William McIlvaine = WM	R. F. Zogbaum = RFZ
E. J. Meeker = EJM	Unidentified = UI

Illustration Source

Battles & Leaders = B & L

The Civil War: The Artists' Record = CWAR

Civil War in Pictures = CWP

Harper's New Monthly Magazine = HNMM

L. Prang & Co. = LP

Leslie's Illustrated Civil War = LICW

Alfred R. Waud, Civil War Artist = AWCWA

LOC = Library of Congress

Acknowledgements

I would like to extend my thanks to Gettysburg Licensed Battlefield Guide John Krohn, M. D., for the advice and encouragement that helped complete this work.

A special thanks is due to Jim Roubal and Dave Weaver, also Licensed Battlefield Guides. After spending many hours of reviewing, Jim and Dave provided a fresh look and assistance by offering suggestions, insights, and pointing out needed corrections. Dave served as an infantry captain in the U. S. Army in Mosul, Iraq and supplied many interesting parallels between today's military experience and soldiers in the Civil War.

Many valuable sources of information were made available through the courtesy of Adams County Library, Gettysburg, Pennsylvania, Gettysburg College Library, including the Special Collections Department, Gettysburg National Military Park, and the University of North Carolina.

Lastly, I must acknowledge the support of my family, particularly my wife and best friend, Diane, who has shown total patience and understanding in the completion of this work and also the continued encouragement from my daughters, Renee and Kerry.

Introduction

Born from the experience of the Civil War was the germination of a ceaseless struggle to determine why and how events happened, to sort out which actions influenced the course of the conflict. As a result, the search has produced the most sweeping study of this important episode, more than any other event in U.S. history.

Every angle, every facet of an action that transpired is thoroughly examined. Discussions proceed incessantly, unabated by time. This quest for certain truths is very much alive today with no end in sight. The phenomenon is indeed quite fortunate. It brings us to new levels of understanding and objectivity about a tragic period that forged our country.

This work hopes to achieve a better understanding of the soldiers' plight in the event—namely, their fears, their stresses, and how they coped. The title, although coined from the comment made by a soldier who fought in World War II about his introduction to battle, could apply to any soldier in any war:

> YOU'LL BE SCARED. Sure, you'll be scared. Before you go into battle, you'll be frightened at the uncertainty, at the thought of being killed. Will it hurt? Will you know what to do?
>
> If you say you're not scared, you'll be a cocky fool. Don't let anyone tell you you're a coward if you admit being scared. Fear before you're actually in the battle is a normal emotional reaction. It's the last step of preparation, the not-knowing, in spite of all that you've learned.
>
> After you've become used to the picture and the sensations of the battlefield, you will change. All the things you were taught in training will come back to you. This is the answer. This is where you will prove that you are a good soldier. That first fight—that fight with yourself—will have gone. Then you will be ready to fight the enemy. [1]

There are few more traumatic experiences than preparing for and engaging in combat. Tension builds. Soldiers are engulfed in an emotionally charged state. Fear of injury or death, of not performing to self-expectations or to the hopes of fellow comrades pervade soldiers' minds while trying to grapple with their circumstance.

The power of fear is an important component in reflecting on how battles are fought—important enough to be considered along with the quantitative data such as the number of artillery pieces and "trigger pullers." Measurable data can infer which side had the advantage. They help support explanations for a battle's outcome. But the elusive forces that caused men to stay on the battle line, to fight defiantly, to pull those triggers, to respond to commands are what swayed battles to and fro and caused successes and failures.

Studying fear is complicated. Each soldier handled challenges in his own way. Each had different limits of physical endurance. Each had different levels of mental discipline to deal with terror and each held a diversity of moral values within the group.

Furthermore, fear is an intangible emotion. Reaction to it is influenced by many abstract elements such as level of morale and motivation. Responses are affected by mental stress, from the duration of exposure to danger, and from the internal conflict between duty and self-preservation.

Fear is affected by elements such as physical stress from fatigue, deprivation of sleep, food, or from unhealthful living. It is also influenced by learned experiences such as cultural values, training, bonds created from common social backgrounds, and group participation. Combined, all these elements and many more control how humans, as individuals and as groups, deal with fear.

The product of being exposed to any or all of the above elements altered paths of logic for decision making. It changed the way in which soldiers managed fear and coped with dangerous situations. These elusive influences are subjective, difficult to assess, and not measurable with any great degree of accuracy.

Intangibles, however, such as a soldier's level of stress, motivation, morale, or state of fear are observable. Stress induced from fatigue, for example, becomes obvious from the appearance of soldiers or their sluggish actions. An increase in numbers of desertions or incidents of disobedience is a measurable value that could be signs of decreased motivation, depressed morale, or overpowering fear. Contemplating the power or value of intangibles as to their contribution is, of course, precarious. Their effects cannot be proven nor can they be disproven. This does not mean that they should be written off or ignored. We cannot deny their influence.

In the pages to follow, fear, what influenced it, and how Civil War soldiers managed to endure through the terrifying experience of combat will be discussed. Most of the story is told in their own riveting words. Officially and unfortunately, little or no attention was devoted towards addressing the effects of fear, how it interfered with performance, and the traumatic consequences created from the experience.

Civil War documentation, provides almost no clinical data on the subject. There were no formal surveys, compilations, or studies regarding reactions before, during, and after combat. To supplement and validate identical emotions that link all combat veterans, some quotes, compilations, and studies were "borrowed" from the experiences of other wars [non-Civil War data are duly noted].

The emotional experiences of soldiers from any war are, nevertheless, universal and timeless. Tactics and the types of stress may have changed, but the emotion of fear remains the same. In fact, one aging war veteran remarked about the resemblance of soldiers between his war and today's: "[They] operate in a manner remarkably reminiscent of the way we fought so many years ago. The similarities are surreal. Close your eyes for a moment, and it all comes rushing back." [2]

Fear:
Meddler and Savior

Fear is contagious but courage is no less so. S. L. A. Marshall [3]

Fear—it's one of the most powerful words in any language. Just the sound of the word registers a mild elevation of emotion within us. It's a feeling caused by anticipation or an awareness of danger and is heightened when reacting to an immediate situation.

Although fear is an unpleasant, often strong, sensation, it provides the most beneficial purpose for any species of living creatures: it warns the senses of potential injury or threat; it directs actions away from perils that may cause harm and, thereby, increases the chance of survival; it allows evolution of the species. It is one of the oldest and strongest emotions of mankind.

Fear originates from several sources. Sometimes the causes are explainable, sometimes not. Some fears we were born with. Many humans, for example, have an innate fear of snakes. They continue to harbor this feeling even though they have no personal experience to justify it.

Some fears are learned. A person, previously bitten by a dog, experiences caution in the presence of canines. There are people that fear sharks, not necessarily because of a personal experience, but because of having viewed a movie about shark attacks.

Fear may also be caused by anxiety. Anxiety is a pervasive apprehension of a threat of danger. It's sometimes defined as a reaction to an imagined danger, while fear is a reaction to real danger.

Other fears, perhaps illogical and amusing to some, may be specialized. These are called phobias. There are many and include such phobias as a fear of itching, fear of streets, and fear of chickens. There's even one, alliumphobia, a fear of garlic.

Leisure Fear

Interestingly, exposure to danger and accompanying fear is exhilarating to most of us in varying degrees. Humans like to place themselves in pretend, staged situations in order to "enjoy" the rush of fear. The experience is called "fun." Staged situations employ a high regard for safety to prevent injury yet they create exciting, sometimes highly expensive, scenarios for thrill-seekers.

Everyone has their own comfort level in which they place themselves to experience "leisure fear." At the timid level, for example, many enjoy roller coaster rides. First, there is the tension-building ride towards the top, followed by the first steep drop, the electrifying few minutes of heart-pounding emotional rushes, the abrupt stop, and, often, the fun-seeker returns to the line to repeat the experience.

Some prefer more exciting experiences by placing themselves in more hazardous situations which, to them, are stimulating, irresistible, and addictive. Skydivers, base jumpers, and mountain climbers fall into this category.

Even Civil War soldiers, like modern day risk-takers, actually "enjoyed" the rush of fear or emotions, not from pretend situations, but those induced from combat. Lieutenant Wheeler, artillery officer, 13th New York Battery, described his experience during the three days at Gettysburg. After exposure to frequent fire and pushed to the limits of physical endurance, he described his feelings as being ones with overriding joy. With the imminent chance of death a constant companion, Wheeler perceived that the "danger was so great and so constant, that it took away the sense of danger" and that this feeling was substituted with "joyous exaltation, a perfect indifference to circumstances." To him it appeared that they were three of the most enjoyable days of his life. Having thought about his experience months later, however, he concluded that his job as battery commander forced his senses to their peak performance in order to achieve success which excited his nerves and senses to their highest level. [4]

True Fear

Fear has its use, but cowardice has none. I may not put my hand into the jaws of a snake, but the very sight of the snake need not strike terror into me. The trouble is that we often die many times before death overtakes us.
Mahatma Gandhi

The opportunities to experience true, justifiable fear exist in no greater calling than the military. The type of fears sought by recreational daredevils mentioned above differs, of course, from soldiers' fears. Thrill-seekers' fears are self-induced, done chiefly for the enjoyment of adrenaline rushes and done voluntarily. For fear induced in combat, the soldiers' plight is different: the probability of death or injury is "the real deal."; men are placed in dangerous situations involuntarily, at the whims of their commanders; they are "trapped" on the battlefield, movements are restricted, thereby the chance to remedy their fears is limited. And Civil War soldiers, unlike modern-day thrill seekers, had their bodies pounded down by extreme physical exertions and deprivations from hard campaigning. Their degraded condition sapped energy and mental capacity to manage emotions.

With regards to modern day warriors, Maj. Gen. Robert H. Scales, U.S. Army, retired, spoke of fear as experienced in Iraq and Afghanistan:

Confederate of 1862
ACR/B & L

> Fear grips every soldier's heart as he closes in on the enemy. Once bullets start flying over his head, he is pulled by two opposing psychological forces. One is fear of violent death and the prospect of dying alone. Psychologists call this phenomenon "palliation." The other is the imperative to follow orders and not let his buddies down. A soldier chooses the latter when he has confidence in his leaders and when he is in touch with those around him. Touch is particularly tough to maintain in the urban terrain of Iraq and Afghanistan...[5]

Undoubtedly, the degree of fear among soldiers varied but all encountered it, sometimes en masse. In describing Wheeler's and Roddey's raid on Rosecrans' communications in 1862, Confederate Col. George B. Hodge, cavalry brigade commander, reported:

> Being ordered by General Davidson to lead them and to take command of the rear in person, I counter-marched with my brigade and was proceeding at a gallop with my command back, when, ahead of me, I encountered the whole of Scott's brigade crowded in frightful and horrible confusion, wild and frantic with panic, choking the entire road and bearing down upon me at racing speed.
>
> It was too late to clear the way; they rode over my command like madmen, some of them stopping only, as I am informed, when they reached the Tennessee. I was ridden over and my horse knocked down, but succeeded in extricating myself and Captain Larmer's company,

Twenty-seventh Virginia Battalion, which I threw into position behind a fence running at right angles with the road, and opened fire upon the enemy, who were fiercely charging the rear of the panic-stricken crowd. [6]

Who were the most vulnerable to fear? Interestingly, many officers in World War I thought that conscripts with lower intellects were better combat soldiers because they were less responsive to fear. Later studies point to a different conclusion: soldiers with greater mental ability have more self-confidence and are better able to deal with the unsettling circumstances surrounding combat. [7]

Post Civil War reactions about the experience felt by soldiers in combat are mixed. So the question often asked veterans by the curious that had not seen combat was "How does it feel to be in battle?" To this question, Confederate artilleryman, Lt. Col. W. T. Poague answered, "Comparatively few men are physical and moral cowards. Even when the courage is wanting, the example and opinion of comrades often acts in place of it. Brave men cheerfully acknowledge their appreciation of the danger." [8]

One Civil War survivor, Allen C. Redwood, replied, "The answer is not so simple as might appear at first sight." He elaborated on his battle inoculation experience with the 55th Virginia at Beaver Dam Creek, June 26, 1862:

> The first engagement [in which he] took a modest part had been entirely foreseen, yet its development refuted all preconceived ideas of what battle was like.
> ….We had formed line on the right of the road and approached the wooded camp-site in which, as we supposed, the foe was concealed and awaiting us. When almost up to it, some excited soldier discharged his musket; at once, and without orders, the entire right wing of the regiment blazed away at the numerous collection of tent-poles and cracker-boxes…At that time there probably was not a Federal soldier nearer than…a mile distant. [9]

Fear can be generated by a complex packet of factors related to physical and mental stresses on the body. Soldiers, especially, are subjected to a multitude of stresses dealing with the rigors of military life: fatigue from mental exertions relating to survival, physical exertions, exposure to weather, and deprivation of the normal needs for living all combine to create a cumulative sway in how to control fear.

Stresses affect the way fear is experienced. They do not necessarily cause it. Major Gregory Daddis, U. S. Army, notes that the "cumulative lack of sleep, combined with other privations such as hunger, affect efficiency on the field of battle and the individual and organizational will to resist fear." The important element to note, then, is that elevated stress alters the way fear is handled. [10]

Fear Triggers

The Logical Trigger: Elements of Prediction

The oldest and strongest emotion of mankind is fear, and the oldest and strongest kind of fear is fear of the unknown. H. P. Lovecraft

Fear can be triggered by digesting information about a situation, perceiving the circumstances, and figuring out a reaction to it. In a military environment, this challenge is especially complicated because of the difficulty in reading situations correctly and where the high stakes penalty for errors in judgment is often death.

After gathering available information, the brain decides on what is dangerous and what is not.   If an outcome is uncertain, the brain is stimulated to seek information and the stress level to predict the best response is heightened.

Digesting information about a situation to achieve the right reaction can be simple. Soldiers immersed in dangerous situations had many visual and aural signals to help interpret what was happening. Ducking bullets when hearing gunfire was, of course, a sane response.

Reactions could be a complex mix of deduction. Author Gavin DeBecker, in his book, *The Gift of Fear*, lists queries the brain uses to help determine an outcome:

1. Measurability—Is it clear what will happen?
2. Vantage—Is the predictor in a position to observe and in context?
3. Imminence—Will it occur soon or a remote time in the future?
4. Context—Is it possible to evaluate the conditions and circumstances?
5. Pre-incident indicators—Are there detectable pre-incident indicators?
6. Experience—Does the person have prior experience to help predict?
7. Comparable events—Can you consider outcomes that are comparable?
8. Objectivity— Is person objective enough to make either outcome possible? [People who believe in only one outcome have completed their prediction.]
9. Investment—To what degree is person invested in the outcome?
10. Replicability—Is it practical to test prediction by trying it first?
11. Knowledge—Does person making prediction have accurate knowledge about the topic? [11]

One of the most important influences in triggering fear was scarcity of information. In battle, ordinary soldiers were generally only mildly aware of their situation. They had few details to gauge their plight. They marched and counter marched around the field with seemingly no purpose or obvious objective. Unexplained actions only prompted the imagination to fill in the blanks, elevating concern for their own survival.

As a result, soldiers, ever since the first armies were formed, make up their own particulars if leaders don't tell them the facts. It is their right to devise their own slant on the state of affairs in the form of speculative guesswork, commonly called rumors. Rumors that the line was giving way, for example, could easily deflate effectiveness and hasten a premature withdrawal or they could initiate an action contrary to the wishes of the commander.

To counter rumors and subdue the mental overload that soldiers experienced, it behooved officers to provide soldiers with as much information as they could. It helped reduce uncertainty and anxiety. One expert noted: "The 'absence of information' is one of the conditions that fosters panic in troops: 'fears arise from matters they don't understand—keep men informed.'" World War II veteran, Lt. Charles Jordan, 9th Division, said, "The absolute worst period of fear came as we were organizing for an attack. We never knew what to expect or when to expect it, and the longer the wait the greater the fear." [12]

The mind's ability to predict and seek a logical outcome was exceptionally difficult in the Civil War. Without smokeless gunpowder, visibility was limited. Smoke from artillery and musket fire blanketed the field. The visual tags that were needed to determine a situation disappeared as a battle's intensity increased. What couldn't be seen was left for the imagination to create a proper response. Hypothesizing on what was happening only heightened the stress level to resolve a problem. Guessing only increased the risk of error. It complicated the reaction by inserting questionable information to obtain a solution that could be deadly if it was wrong.

Soldiers with lively imaginations, then, were found to be more susceptible to fears. As danger increases, fear may escalate into panic. When this happens, thought deteriorates into distorted mental images, into complete irrationality. Soldiers, just a few of them, overwhelmed with anxiety and unable to cope with stress during a fight, could ruin a situation—even one that had promise to succeed. Vietnam veteran Lieutenant Philip Caputo, U.S. Marine Corps, observed that "a man needs many things in war, but a strong imagination is not one of them. In Vietnam, the best soldiers were usually unimaginative men who did not feel afraid until there was obvious reason." [13]

When senses are elevated to their keenest edge, every sound, every glimpse, and every stir was taken in to calculate the situation and prepare a response for contact with the enemy. "The cold fear of violent death and the prospect of killing another human being," according to one modern-day veteran, "heighten the senses, sear these experiences deeply and irrevocably into our souls, and linger in the back recesses of our minds…For whatever primal reason, we see sharper, we hear more clearly, and develop a sixth sense about everything around us." [14]

This elevated state of awareness sometimes, however, bred over-caution. Second Lieutenant John Calef, 2nd U.S. Artillery, noted the alert state of preparedness exhibited by his men in anticipation of the coming action against

Battle of Winchester. *JET/LICW*

Confederate forces: "…Alarmed by the sound of firing as if between pickets on our right and front; battery got ready for action, expecting an immediate attack; proved to be infantry firing off their muskets to clean them." [15]

At night, especially, it was not unusual for overcautious sentries and pickets to fire at shadows or suspicious movements. Col. Rufus Dawes of the 6th Wisconsin, Iron Brigade, described one instance: "It is a troubled and dreamy sleep at best that comes to the soldier on a battlefield. About one o'clock at night we had a great alarm. A man in the Seventh Indiana Regiment, next on our right, cried so loudly in his sleep that he aroused all the troops in the vicinity. Springing up, half bewildered, I ordered my regiment to 'fall in,' and a heavy fire of musketry broke out from along the whole line of men."[16]

Imagination, Information, Perception

Fear makes men forget, and skill which cannot fight, is useless.
—Phormio of Athens

If imagination didn't engender fear in combat, it skewed perception and, at least, added stress to seek solutions to the situation. Perceptions of situations may, in fact, be totally false because of incorrect data, insufficient or conflicting information, or inaccurate predictions. The reaction to perceptions, nevertheless, is real.

Civil War soldiers in a battle line, for example, including officers and unit commanders, often moved to instructions from higher commands. Orders to maneuver, more often than not, were general in nature. They were simple instructions passed on verbally or scribbled on paper. The purpose of such orders might have no specific goal other than to strengthen the line, to exploit an advantage, or to position manpower to await further use. They frequently excluded the purpose of the move, its intentions, or its goals.

At Gettysburg on July 2nd, Union Gen. Slocum sent Gen. Williams to lead the 1st division, 12th Corps, to help shore up the collapsing Union left:

After striking the Taneytown road, we passed large gatherings of our troops swarming in confusion on the easterly slopes of the ridge, apparently recently driven back. A Staff officer of Gen. Slocum started with me, but he had no information as to what point reinforcements were needed, nor could anyone among the swarming fugitives tell me where I could find a corps commander or any organized body of our troops, to which I could unite my reinforcements. We were met with loud cheers and shouts to "go on and give them Jessie" but nobody seemed to know where to go in, nor did any of them offer to go in with us. [17]

In the same corps, Gen. John Geary's 2nd division also received useless instructions regarding this move. "When ordered thus to leave my entrenchments," Geary said, "I received no specific instructions as to the object of the move, the direction to be taken, or the point to be reached, beyond the order to move, by the right flank and to follow the First Division." [18]

In a Confederate example, on July 2nd, Major General Richard H. Anderson, 3rd Corps division commander, reported the lack of information and the short notice he received to implement his attack orders:

Shortly after the line had been formed, I received notice that Lieutenant-General Longstreet [1st Corps], would occupy the ground on the right; that his line would be in a direction nearly at right angles with mine; that he would assault the extreme left of the enemy and drive him toward Gettysburg, and I was at the same time ordered to put the troops of my division into action by brigades as soon as those of General Longstreet's corps had progressed so far in their assault as to be connected with my right flank. [19]

The mission assigned to Anderson was not explicit enough to let him know the precise object of the attack and provided little understanding in recognizing whether the attack before him was going as planned or was a deviation from it. His attack could be characterized more as one of blind purpose than a deliberate and skilled cooperative action trying to outmaneuver the enemy. [Today's army emphasizes "task and purpose" in conveyance of orders so as to avoid such confusion.]

Adding to the confusion, higher commands issued orders from data that could be inaccurate, obsolete, or from fragmentary pieces of information reported by others. The assumption that leaders knew all and issued orders accordingly is a myth. Soldiers, nevertheless, trusted leaders with their lives. They expected their commanders to be skilled "tabernacles of wisdom" and issue orders based on sound information and good judgment. Any visual signals viewed by troops indicating confusion among generals only stirred up fears in the ranks.

But officers could not always readily calculate their situation. Union Maj.

Gen. Abner Doubleday, division commander at Gettysburg, once aptly remarked: "People are very much mistaken when they suppose because a man is in battle he knows all about it." "It is difficult in the excitement of a battle," he noted, "to see everything going on around us for each has his own part to play and that absorbs his attention to the exclusion of everything else." [20]

Col. John M. Stone, commanding the 2nd Mississippi in the railroad cut, recollected about the 1st day's action to his commander, Brig. Gen. Joseph R. Davis:

> ...The 1st day is vague and indistinct. I was very much like the French soldier of whom you sometimes told us, who never saw anything while the battle was going on except the rump of his fat file leader. In battle, I rarely knew anything that occurred beyond the immediate vicinity of my own command. In battle when I commanded a company, it engaged my whole attention, when a regiment, I knew little of any other command, and so on....I received my orders from you, and do not remember that I was made acquainted with the orders issuing to brigade commanders by Gen. Heth. [21]

Conflicting and confusing orders, or ones lacking information, added to misperceptions of the situation. Such directives placed an immense mental burden on officers and men trying to obey commands. Just before the battle of Five Forks, Joshua Chamberlain wrote, "Within the space of two hours, Warren (commanding the Union 5th Corps) received orders involving important movements for his entire corps, in four different directions. These came in rapid succession…The orders which came to General Warren that night were to an amazing degree confused and conflicting." [22]

Even firsthand observations could be deceptive as to what was actually happening. Replacing men on a battle line in the midst of an engagement, for example, was an important and sensitive maneuver. This action was termed "the passage of lines." The orchestration of exchanging men on the line was one of the most critical transitions of a battle. If this could be done with precision, a newly formed group of men could quickly replace the worn out and deranged mob and continue the fight. The degree of difficulty in a transition, however, depended on the size of the units and the fight's intensity. Exchanging large units during intense fighting at close range was exceptionally difficult to pull off and increased the risk of disaster.

In the normal course of battle, men stayed on the line because everyone else stayed there. But seeing men from other units moving to the rear and not realizing they were simply being replaced by fresh troops created an instant and unnerving feeling. For the replacements coming in, a chaotic passage of lines was just as unnerving. A confused mass of soldiers moving off the line, especially at a hastened pace, could instantly "contaminate" those going into action and destroy their resolve. [23]

Misperception through gross overstatement of the enemy's strength was another way to instill fear resulting in serious consequences. In the Maryland campaign, September, 1862, Confederate Maj. Gen. Daniel H. Hill, commanding division, reported:

> Yankee columns were allowed to come within easy range, when a sudden storm of grape and canister drove them back in confusion. Betts' men must have given them a very hot fire, as Burnside reported that he had met three heavy columns on the hill. It is difficult to imagine how 30 men could so multiply themselves as to appear to the frightened Yankees to be three heavy columns. [24]

Concerned about misinformation on enemy strengths through overinflated reports from forward outposts, Maj. Gen. Hooker, commander of the Army of the Potomac issued General Order No. 40:

> The outposts of an army are its safeguards, and this duty must be so performed that the camps are not unnecessarily disturbed. Officers of outposts are expected to inform themselves accurately of all events transpiring in their vicinity, and those whose fears magnify trifling squads into large bodies of the enemy as richly deserve death as the base wretch who deserts his country's flag or his comrades in battle.
>
> It has been too much a practice, upon outposts and battle-fields, to send back reports and calls for re-enforcements, founded upon imagination or the tales of a frightened or cowardly shirk. The fate of battle may be changed by such reports.
>
> Officers will be held responsible that their reports from the front are perfectly reliable. Their attention is called to the Forty-ninth Article of War. Corps and division commanders are required to see that any officer or soldier, guilty of conduct in conflict with its provisions, or of the character referred to in this order, is brought before a court-martial without delay. [25]

Symptoms of Fear

Fear, once triggered, prepares the body for action. Physical symptoms appear. The senses increase in awareness to gather more information for an imminent response. In *Acts of War*, veterans described their personal observations regarding fear in battle. The author wrote: "(For most soldiers) fear is present to a greater or lesser degree, and may be experienced as anything from mild apprehension to paralyzing terror. Its physical symptoms are well documented, and one does not have to have survived battle to have experienced at least the most moderate of them."

"A violent pounding of the heart is the most common…" but they also include

Forward Union picket post. *AB/CWAR*

"a sinking feeling in the stomach, uncontrollable trembling, a cold sweat, a feeling of weakness or stiffness and vomiting." A small percentage, 5 or 6%, in interviews with soldiers of more recent wars, involuntarily urinated or defecated.

"Losing control of bladder or bowels are the symptoms of fear which tend to be most unwelcome, primarily because of the cultural taboos surrounding these bodily functions, and, of course, because they are difficult to conceal." [26]

In World War II, reactions to fear were reported by troops in four combat divisions in April, 1944:

Symptoms	Avg. % Experiencing Symptom
Violent pounding of heart	76%
Sinking feeling in the stomach	63%
Shaking or trembling all over	52%
Feeling sick at the stomach	48%
Cold sweat	46%
Feeling of stiffness	41%
Feeling of weakness or feeling faint	41%

Symptoms	Avg. % Experiencing Symptom
Vomiting	19%
Losing control of bowels	12%
Urinating in pants	7% [27]

First Action

Courage is doing what you're afraid to do. There can be no courage unless you're scared. Eddie Rickenbacher

The ability to manage fear was especially unpredictable for soldiers uninitiated to battle. No one was born a veteran. The first experience was considered to be a soldier's greatest test as a warrior. In World War I, Captain J. E. H. Neville, in a letter to his family, shared his deep personal thoughts about going into battle for the first time: "The only thing I'm not certain about is whether I may get the wind up and show it. I'm afraid of being afraid." [28]

For the uninitiated ones, entry into the first battle could be imagined, but not accurately. One Confederate officer observed the metamorphosis of one man in his unit from novice to veteran:

[This man] ...who helped to rally the Texans and Georgians on the 10th of May at Spottsylvania, [was] first exhorting them as "gentlemen," then berating and belaboring them as "cowards."

No man who was ever in the Howitzers but will appreciate the grim absurdity of this man's feeling a lack of confidence in his own nerve and courage; but he did feel it.

When the war broke out he was in Europe enjoying himself, but returned to his native State, serving first in some, as he considered it, "non-combatant" position, until that became unendurable to him, and then he joined the Howitzers as a private soldier; and that final flurry of the 10th of May was the first real fight he ever got into.

Hearing someone say just as it was over that it had been "pretty hot work," he asked with the greatest earnestness whether the speaker really meant what he said, and when assured that he did, he asked two or three others of his comrades, whom he regarded as experienced soldiers, whether they concurred in this view of the matter, and on their expressing emphatic concurrence, he expressed intense satisfaction at having at last a standard in his mind, and a relieving standard at that; saying that he had feared he would disgrace his family by exhibiting a lack of courage; but if this was really "hot work," he felt that he would be able to maintain himself and do his duty.

The story is almost too much for belief, but it is the sober truth and vouched for by gentlemen of the highest character. [29]

While some were elated to have successfully passed their trial, for many, their first experience was upsetting. Some experienced the involuntary physical reactions as mentioned above. They did not yet realize that their response was not only normal but actually very common. Only additional experience would overcome self-disappointment and reassure them of this.

Every soldier has a different capacity to deal with fear. Depending on the individual, reactions to fear may elicit varied responses in identical situations. A soldier with an unswayable character, for example, would react differently than a weaker-willed person under the same pressure.

Additionally, everyone's capacity to manage fear is not a static condition, making each new experience unpredictable. It is a myth that once soldiers became battle-hardened veterans they would do well in future clashes. A soldier viewed by others as courageous, for example, because of his steadfastness in battle, may eventually reach a breaking point from the perpetual exposure to danger.

Injury and death surround men in battle. Extended periods of fighting increased the feeling of gloom, a sense of endlessness to the conflict, and the inevitability of death. Fear of physical harm, understandably, creates an overwhelming level of anxiety. Exhaustion and hopelessness sometimes led to heroic actions. Some had reached a point where despair coaxed men into reckless behavior to get death over with. [30]

A survey of wounded combat veterans in the European Theater during World War II is telling. Of the 277 soldiers interviewed, "65 percent of the men admitted having had at least one experience in combat in which they were unable to perform adequately because of intense fear." [31]

In the Civil War, an officer in the Army of Northern Virginia said: "...Every soldier of experience knows that when a man has reached a certain point of demoralization and until he has settled down again past that point, it is absolutely useless to attempt to rouse him to a sense of duty or of honor. I have seen many a man substantially in the condition of the fellow who, as he executed a flying leap over the musket of the guard threatening to shoot and crying 'Halt!'—called back, 'Give any man fifty dollars to halt me, but can't halt myself!'" [32]

At the battle of Pittsburg Landing, or Shiloh, Tenn. in 1862, Union Brig. Gen. William Nelson, commanding Fourth Division, reported :

I found cowering under the river bank when I crossed from 7,000 to 10,000 men, frantic with fright and utterly demoralized, who received my gallant division with cries, "We are whipped; cut to pieces." They were insensible to shame or sarcasm--for I tried both on them--and, indignant at such poltroonery, I asked permission to open fire upon the knaves. [In his report, Gen. Nelson did not mention the result of his request.] [33]

Fear Responses

A running soldier cannot be stopped... [34]

Everyone has experienced fear in one form or another, whether it is mild caution or an acute type described as petrified terror. Extreme forms in civilian life, such as automobile accidents and violent crimes, have produced symptoms similar to those of combat veterans. But unless one "has seen the elephant," an accurate supposition of what the emotional experience of battle was like can only be imagined as a stereotyped version by those who have never dealt intimately with such an event.

Responses to fear, however, are not necessarily relative to the situation. Just the perception of danger may overwhelm a person to the point of making irrational choices and abnormal behavior. A person afraid of mice, for example, may jump on a chair and freeze in fright at the site of the rodent scurrying across the kitchen floor, even though that person knows darn well that mice don't attack and harm people. Although this response may seem trivial, the fear expressed, nevertheless is real to that individual.

To cite another example, a lady discovered a large snake coiled under her bed [this happened to a relative] and responded with understandable fright plus added the insistence to replace all the bedclothes. The fear reaction, in this case, is more understandable. Besides the innate dread of these creatures, snakes do attack when cornered, some are poisonous, and hence, the perceived danger is justified.

The Supreme Dilemma

Some have been thought brave because they were afraid to run away.
Ralph Waldo Emerson

For soldiers, the triggers for fear are numerous and justifiable. Fear in combat takes on a different dimension. Reactions address real and highly dangerous situations with the probability that death or injury will result. This mental pressure is coupled with the supreme dilemma of the willingness to sacrifice versus the innate desire for self-preservation. This inner struggle is within every soldier in which the fundamental will to survive competes with devotion to duty.

Historian John Keegan notes, "What battles have in common is human: the behaviour of men struggling to reconcile their instinct for self-preservation, their sense of honour and the achievement of some aim over which other men are ready to kill them. The study of battle is therefore always a study of fear and usually of courage." [35]

Col. Samuel H. Hays and Lt. Col. William N. Thomas, in *Taking Command,* acknowledge "that the soldier lives with continual conflicts; he has a desire to conquer the enemy and a fear of combat. He is pulled between the desire to escape a given dangerous situation and the fear of being considered a coward...Consistent uncertainty is a source of fear in the combat soldier. In fact, the normal state of the soldier is one of fear and fatigue." [36]

Understanding Fear

Courage is resistance to fear, mastery of fear-not absence of fear. Except a creature be part coward it is not a compliment to say it is brave.
Lucius Annaeus Seneca

Fear is generally associated with weakness. But this is too harsh an assessment. Reacting to fear is merely a practical emotion to avoid injury and prolong one's life. A person exposed to danger without experiencing fear to steer an action away from peril would not last long in a combat situation. "Fearless" soldiers either wasted their own lives, perhaps needlessly, or jeopardized those around them. There is at least one instance in World War II, at the Battle of the Bulge, where an out-of-control machine gunner was shot by his own men because he jeopardized the safety of the whole group by refusing to stop firing. There were heroes, however, that sacrificed their lives for a purpose. In these cases, determination, or an overriding concern for comrades superseded personal fear. [37]

The opposite of fear, then, is not fearlessness. Fearlessness is performing in battle with a total disregard for personal safety. World War II veteran, Lt. Charles Jordan, 9th Division, wrote:

I have read of fearless people, I even had a runner for a short time who I think was pretty close to fearless (he got killed), but I was not fearless. My worst fear was of screwing up or showing my fear to those around me. A distant second was fear of death. In my early days this included the fear of being wounded but this rapidly transformed into a desire. [38]

In this context, the antonym for fear is not fearlessness but "courage"—the ability to manage fear and perform under fire. Taken a step further, exceptional performance in combat is "bravery" or, in today's military terminology— "valor."

Gen. George Patton gave his take on bravery and courage by saying:

If we take the generally accepted definition of bravery as a quality which knows not fear, I have never seen a brave man. All men are frightened. The more intelligent they are, the more they are frightened. The courageous man is the man who forces himself, in spite of his fear, to carry on. Discipline, pride, self-respect, self-confidence, and the love of glory are attributes which will make a man courageous even when he is afraid. [39]

In his work *Gettysburg: A Meditation on War and Values,* Kent Gramm, described fear and courage:

> As courage is the primary virtue, cowardice is the primary vice. But fear is our ruling passion—our primary passion; it stands behind all the others that endanger us.
> A person who is afraid, really afraid, is capable of anything, and will do it to anyone, including and perhaps especially, those closest—wives, husbands, and children. These are the easiest and softest targets—and when a person is afraid it is exactly such a target he or she wants. Ethics, reason, practicality are alike taken under the rule and into the service of this passion. Hunger, lust, all the drives give way to abject fear. Only love seems to be resistant, because it is willing to forget the basis of fear: self-preservation. Thus courage is born. [40]

Civilized states have flourished or failed through their performance on the battlefield. Convincing humans to engage opponents in order to perpetuate one's culture or save its society is a fascinating and primeval concept. It rests on the notion that there are members of society willing to sacrifice themselves for a higher cause. Where would those cultures be, the ones which have lasted through the ages, without the overriding desire of its citizens to preserve their way of life? Or, putting it in another way, where would war be without the ability to ignite this willingness to sacrifice? This willingness depends immensely on persuading people to overcome their innate desire for self-preservation and choose the most dangerous path by engaging in mortal combat.

Courage vs. Cowardice

The bravest are surely those who have the clearest vision of what is before them, glory and danger alike, and yet notwithstanding go out to meet it.
Thucydides

Fear is openly expressed by some and culturally concealed by most. It is human nature, especially males, to intentionally hide submissive body language in a confrontation and, instead, put on the "game face." Wincing in a showdown or "blinking" when staring down an opponent, for example, indicates acquiescence and only emboldens an opponent to respond with an offensive reaction.

In combat, concealing fear is especially important. The ability to manage fear and perform was an admirable way of gaining mutual respect from fellow soldiers. Performing under fire is the critical measurement which distinguishes courage from cowardice. World War II veteran, John Watney, described his inner struggle to overcome his fear and not shame himself in front of his comrades: "I was a coward; and the thing I feared more than anything in the world was to break up in battle and give way to that cowardice...; I prayed, until a lump came into my throat, to be spared that degradation." [41]

Private Carlton McCarthy of the Richmond Howitzers spoke about the expectations for a soldier: "In a thousand ways he is tried . . . every quality is put to the test. If he shows the least cowardice he is undone. His courage must never fail. He must be manly and independent." The "dash" instilled in these motivated young men, however, quickly subsided from their exposure to the sobering horrors of warfare surrounding them. [42]

The terms "courage" and "cowardice," however, have different meanings across time, both culturally and medically. They must be critiqued in context with the period in which they happened. We, who were raised and nourished in a modern day society are a product of contemporary thought and experience. Our daily judgments and senses are based on personal knowledge. We interpret things differently than those living in another century in judging their values, tolerations, and condemnations.

We are, therefore, susceptible to being trapped into false conclusions by interpreting mid-nineteenth century virtues, values, and shortcomings in terms of acceptable rules that embrace today's society. Likewise, if those living in days long gone viewed society today, it would appear our lives are governed in a manner that is foreign, futuristic, and radical to their experiences.

Consequently, we view each war with a different and defined set of effects on its soldiers. Judging the cultural rules of behavior in the Civil War, for example, was partially based on the lack of medical advancement in recognizing mental trauma caused from combat. The science of psychiatry did not exist. For those that were mentally "wounded," failure to control fear, the inability to perform duties, or "copping out" on fellow soldiers, then, was viewed more as a character flaw than a mental condition. Today, rather than being scorned as a personality defect, the military actually recognizes and classifies this condition of mental stress as an injury. A great deal of attention, research, and treatment is devoted to treating this stress disorder. [43]

Each war is also viewed with its own set of circumstances that call for courageous actions that may not be appropriate in other conflicts. Hundreds of Civil War soldiers, for example, have been praised, promoted, and awarded the highest medals for saving or capturing flags. The flag, although highly revered today, was, back then, equivalent to a religious icon, a symbol representing a culture or a cause, and worthy of giving one's life to save it. Many, in fact, died in the process. They were, no doubt, courageous.

Sergeant William H. Green, Thirty-seventh Wisconsin, Company C, for example, was "recommended for promotion for gallantry in action, Petersburg, Va., June 17, 1864, where he was wounded in both legs,... he [then] crawled

from the field, dragging his colors with his teeth; died July 17, 1864, of wounds."
[44]

Such heroic actions regarding flags in modern military culture are virtually non-existent. Comparatively, flags play a smaller role in today's unit operations and opportunities for such actions are greatly diminished. The colors during the Civil War were often in the midst of the action, in the immediate vicinity of the enemy, and susceptible to capture.

Fighting for the colors. *UI/CWAR*

Judging soldiers' reactions to combat across different wars is also comparatively difficult to reconcile and poses many questions. In the Civil War setting, for example, officers were able to prod thousands of men to cross open fields in the face of the enemy. This was a battle tactic accepted by ordinary soldiers and, at minimum, courageous. Today, such an action would be judged imbecilic. Could we, in fact, coax today's soldiers to do the same? If not, are they less courageous? Was life less important to Civil War soldiers than today's servicemen?

One way to validate soldiers' courage was getting wounded. It demonstrated valor and an injury was physical proof of sacrifice. It initiated them into the community of wounded warriors. Many young soldiers, despite the well-known life-threatening dangers of Civil War medical treatment, willfully tried to get wounded to prove themselves. The title of Stephen Crane's book, *The Red Badge of Courage,* symbolizes the battle wound as passage into the respected brotherhood of brave soldiers. Today the Purple Heart medal transfers the same respect to such men of sacrifice.

Some "old-timers" had different motives for wishing to get wounded. Everyone had a breaking point. Worn down and used up from previous hard combat, veteran soldiers exhibited the same symptoms of fear during and after situations that were not really dangerous. An injury was a pass to safety without the loss of honor and pride. The term "million dollar wound" was coined in World War II to describe a wound that was not life-threatening, but one that would send the soldier home or at least to the rear. In that war, battle veterans "found combat increasingly frightening and often admitted that they *hoped for a wound* in order to have an *honorable* reason for leaving battle." [45]

There is no absolute classification of soldiers as being courageous or cowards. The courageous ones, more or less, were those that remained on the line and did what they were told. The "cowards" either fled and even some might have stayed on the field but feigned injuries to get out of the action.

In one case at Gettysburg, as the 76th New York moved near the railroad, Captain Herschel Pierce of Company A noticed a soldier "nicely rolled up in a blanket," lying behind a stone wall with his head covered up. For a dead man, it seemed unusual. Pierce decided to check it out further. The man was, in fact, very much alive. "What are you doing here?" roared Pierce. "Get up!" "I can't. I am awfully wounded," came the forsaken answer from under the blanket. "Where?" asked the captain. "Here," said the man, pointing to his side. Pierce could find no evidence of blood or injury. The man said he must have been mistaken and pointed to a different place on his body, but, again, Pierce could see no injury. The "wounded" man pointed to several more locations until Pierce shouted, "Get up, you coward! Fall in!" While the malingerer was not in the 76th, Pierce made sure he was in the heaviest fighting for the rest of the day. [46]

Some "cowards" may have disappeared from the field altogether. The urge for self-preservation was stronger than duty to the cause or to their comrades. In the Civil War, compared to today's combat environment, it was relatively easy to leave the battle line through the smoke and chaos by disappearing into the crowds of walking wounded trudging to the rear. Fleeing satisfied the soldier's urge for self-preservation and the relief was immediate, even though the consequences might later lead to execution for desertion. [Desertion levels on both sides were high throughout the war, making the deterrent threat of execution ineffective. Available estimates place Union desertion at 200,000 and Confederate desertion 104,000.] [47]

Escaping the dangers of combat might have been unforgivable by fellow soldiers, but at least, it was understandable. For commanders, ignoring desertions could never be tolerated, otherwise, the prospect of keeping men on the line or conducting a successful operation would be impossible.

Stress:
Damaging and Debilitating

It is easy to be brave from a safe distance. Aesop

Stress is defined as a physical or emotional factor that causes bodily or mental tension. It affects the way fear is experienced and how it is managed or resisted. Reactions to fear among individuals may be different because of variations in stress levels. It is, therefore, important to consider how it modified reactions.

Stress can be triggered from many sources. They include physical exertions and mental pressures arising from dealing with dangerous or unpleasant situations. It is triggered through observation of the senses. Non-military aural stresses, for example, could be caused by the sound of a dentist's drill, fingernails scraped across a blackboard [no one knows why this is abhorrent], or the sound of a baby crying [the level of stress is determined by the intensity].

The stimulus that causes stress, called a stressor, initiates a chain reaction which activates the nervous system and causes the release of stress hormones. The release affects many of the body's functions including dilating pupils, elevating blood sugar, constricting arterioles [small terminal twigs of arteries] in the skin and gut while dilating arterioles in leg muscles, and has a suppressive effect on the immune system.

For higher levels of stress, symptoms from the release include increased heartbeat and breathing, dry mouth, motor agitation, sweating, pallor, enlarged pupils, relaxation of the bladder, and insomnia. Blood flow is diverted to the large muscles to prepare the body for a violent muscular reaction and a corresponding decrease to the digestive system and other organs that are not needed in the response. This will happen even though a response does not call for any physical exertion.

The chief stress hormone released, adrenaline, is secreted directly into the bloodstream. Its reaction occurs within seconds. This discharge causes a response by throwing the body out of balance and forces an action to suppress the stimulus. A worker, for example, who is late in commuting to a meeting to deliver an important presentation, experiences a stressor that triggers a reaction to speed to the engagement as a remedy to the situation.

Adrenalin is the catalyst that gives the body superior power to cause a response beyond one that is solely based on a decision from logic. Most of us have heard about the person who attained "superhuman" strength from adrenaline in order to lift up a car and save an unfortunate victim. [48]

According to Dr. David Harrison:

> Adrenaline has the ability to increase speed and strength. It also decreases how much people feel pain. A large amount of adrenaline released into your system all at once causes what is often called an adrenaline dump, rush, or surge. All of these effects are designed to prepare your body either to run away or to fight…Adrenaline can make you feel energized, or it can make you feel shaky, weak or sick to your stomach. Sometimes all of these feelings come at the same time, which can be confusing. Results of an adrenaline surge might also include:
>
> • feeling as though time has slowed down.
> • tunnel vision, where you only see what is in front of you and not what is around you.
> • a sensation of your mind wandering or floating, making it hard to concentrate.
> • decreased coordination.
> • difficulty in thinking clearly. [49]

Adrenaline reactions depend on how they are triggered. Surprise attacks or unexpected events, for example, cause a natural reaction to freeze, jump, flinch, or run. Before adrenalin takes effect, however, you have already moved or remained still. The adrenalin reinforces the initial response: someone throws a shoe at you, you duck before the adrenalin caused that reaction.

If a reaction is to freeze, it is difficult to convert immobility into action, especially when the adrenalin surge overwhelms an individual to misinterpret the experience to be associated with fear or panic. Fear and panic causes helplessness when action, instead of freezing, is critical to protect oneself or others. Author William Manchester recollected his paralyzing fear while fighting in the Pacific during World War II: "A fresh fear was creeping over my mind, quietly, stealthily, imperceptibly. I sat up; my muscles rippling with suppressed panic." [50]

In many cases, adrenalin improves performance. There are many examples of men executing deeds requiring increased energy to fight harder, to run faster, or

Battery in action. WT/*B & L*

to exhibit "superhuman strength" just mentioned. At Gettysburg on July 2nd, for example, men performed a tremendous feat of muscle power in placing two 1 ½-ton cannons of Lt. Charles Hazlett's Union battery on the crest of Little Round Top. Up the steep slopes, dotted with immovable boulders, the guns "had been lifted, pushed, and pulled into position by cannoneers and infantrymen borrowed for the work. Even General Warren was said to have lent a hand." [51]

On the other hand, adrenaline can degrade dexterity by causing an increase in activities as to make animated movements to be uncoordinated, frantic, or flailing about with little effect. Decreased motor skills, undoubtedly contributed to improper or poor handling of weapons and ammunition. Archeological evidence supports this. Many, if not most, bullets in artifact collections and excavated around many battlefields are unfired "drops." While many cartridges were spilled onto the ground during action or disposed of because of moisture damage, the effects of adrenaline releases, as well, point to fumbling ammunition during loading.

Furthermore, while musket fire caused most Civil War battle casualties, accuracy in combat is overstated. It is often said that a trained Civil War soldier can fire a musket up to three aimed shots per minute. Perhaps this is true in an unstressed situation or where the atmosphere is clear enough to see targets.

Statistics, however, do not support the effort required to achieve this feat. Soldiers, in fact, missed most of the time. At Gettysburg, for example, the combined weight of expended ammunition, bullets and artillery projectiles, was 569 tons. Using a rough estimate, this means that over thirty pounds of ammunition was used *just* to hurt someone. Granted, smoke, trees, or the protection of defense works were major causes that blocked projectiles from hitting targets. Decreased motor skills, undoubtedly, affected aiming as well but, unfortunately, cannot be proven.

Poor visibility or objects that stopped bullets, however, didn't interfere with handling, loading, and firing weapons. In this regard, we do know how soldiers performed. After the battle of Gettysburg, 28,000 muskets were picked up off the field. Some 24,000 were still loaded. Most were loaded wrong: 12,000 had two bullets in them [these are single-shot muskets], 6,000 had from three to ten bullets, some were loaded backwards—the bullet was put in first, then the powder.

The majority of soldiers at Gettysburg were by no means inexperienced. Many had fought in major battles and fired their weapons hundreds of times. It leads to the conclusion that other factors, including adrenalin dumps causing a decrease in motor skills, are responsible for interrupting the ability to perform trained loading motions in sequence. Considering the number of muskets in the battle [roughly 150,000] and the improperly loaded weapons not left on the field for examination, the mis-loads happened on a phenomenal scale.

Adrenaline rushes, then, require soldiers to recognize the effects of their excitement, that their body is involuntarily reacting to an exceptional situation, and to conduct themselves with an immense amount of concentration and self-control in order to perform their duties under fire. Veteran soldiers, compared to uninitiated ones, were, of course, more prone to dealing effectively during such surges.

Although the stress response during emergency measures is, undoubtedly, both vital and valuable, it can also be disruptive and damaging. Most humans rarely encounter emergencies that require physical effort, yet our biology still provides for them. Thus we may find our stress response activated in situations where physical action is inappropriate or even illegal. This activation eventually takes a toll on both our bodies and our minds.

Prolonged experiences of stress responses may result in chronic suppression of the immune system, leaving the sufferer vulnerable to infection by bacteria and viruses. Dr. Ranit Mishori, a modern day expert on stress, noted the increasing connection between stress and illness: "Stress affects your heart, weight, and skin. It's also linked to "poorer wound healing, an increased risk for developing depression, the common cold, and influenza…Ongoing stress…influences your abilities to function and may lower your immunity." [Perhaps immunity suppression contributed to the large number of Civil War deaths from disease and blocked the recuperation of battle injuries.]

Repeated stress responses can be caused not only by real threats, but also by mental disorders such as post-traumatic stress disorder in which the individual shows a stress response when remembering a past trauma and also panic disorder, in which the stress response is activated apparently by nothing. [52]

Stress in the Military

From a military perspective, studies have identified many types of mental and physical stressors created from exertion, deprivation, prolonged exposure to the elements, and to danger. Stressors are a culmination of numerous environmental and operational factors which can erode combat effectiveness. The list of stress factors relating to soldiers is long. A study from World War II identified many:

> [The]main types of stress in combat, not necessarily in order [are]: threats of life and health, physical discomfort from lack of shelter, excessive heat or cold, moisture, dryness, inadequacy of food, water, clothing, from insects, disease, filth, injuries from wounds, long continued fatigue, and lack of sleep. Also, [they include] deprivation of sexual satisfaction, isolation from accustomed sources of affectual assurance, restriction of personal movement by orders or under fire, continual uncertainty and lack of adequate cognitive orientation….lack of privacy, incessant demands and petty irritations of close living within the group,…long periods of enforced boredom, mingled with anxiety between actions,...lack of terminal individual goals; poverty and uncertainty of individual rewards. [53]

Civil War soldiers could relate to any or all the above. A Confederate officer gave his view of the surrounding stresses towards the end of the war when trench warfare was common:

> One can readily understand, now, the supreme discomfort and even suffering of "the lines." Thousands of men cramped up in a narrow trench, unable to go out, or to get up, or to stretch or to stand, without danger to life and limb; unable to lie down, or to sleep, for lack of room and pressure of peril; night alarms, day attacks, hunger, thirst, supreme weariness, squalor, vermin, filth, disgusting odors everywhere; the weary night succeeded by the yet more weary day; the first glance over the way, at day dawn, bringing the sharpshooter's bullet singing past your ear or smashing through your skull, a man's life often exacted as the price of a cup of water from the spring. [54]

Effects of Physical Stress

Activity in war is movement in a resistant medium. Von Clausewitz [55]

The physical demands of combat, hard marching, and the lack of sleep, combined with the adrenaline rushes used up in the excitement of battle, drained the body of its ability to stir and numbed the senses of soldiers. Bodies automatically switched to a stand-by mode to recover what their energy reserves spent in hurried marches or the frantic activities of battle. Fatigued bodies transformed reasoning minds towards incoherence, subdued awareness of reality, and entered into a trance-like world. This exhausted state translated into confusion, incorrect execution of orders, faulty communications, and poor performance.

Commanders knew the importance of a healthy, rested army and the dangers associated with one in an exhausted state. In referring to the Atlanta campaign of 1864, Surgeon Henry S. Hewit, U.S. Army, Medical Director spoke of the army's need to maintain a conscientious approach regarding the physical well-being of its soldiers:

> ...The most important of all reforms...is in the state and condition of the common soldier. It is of absolute importance that line and company officers be taught to take an interest in the physical well-being of their men; that the load that the soldier is required to carry be lightened; that the length and rapidity of marches be diminished; that regularity and quality of food be secured, and sufficient time for rest and recuperation afforded.
>
> The average capability and endurance are gauged by the strongest man in the command, and the rapidity with which the horse of the commanding officer can walk, made the standard for the marching of the soldier, overloaded with knapsack, musket, ammunition, and rations, and frequently intrenching tools superadded.
>
> A system which will secure to the soldier the highest physical development of which he is capable will render forced marches easy of accomplishment when they become necessary. Troops in a high state of health and strength can endure occasional drafts upon their endurance without detriment.
>
> The advantages in a military point of view are obvious. I offer it as my deliberate opinion, based on three years of the most ample experience, that the rapidity and length of marches, and the load which the soldier carries, have more to do with depleting our armies than all other causes put together.
>
> The field, instead of being the school for the highest form of physical training and muscular development, is a treadmill in which the weak and delicate are infallibly destroyed, and the most robust gradually reduced to their capital stock of health and strength, and finally compelled to succumb....
>
> The want of intelligent care and conservation of the private soldier has had more to do with the prolongation of the war and the mishaps which have occurred than any one or any series of causes combined. If our men

had been kept at this normal standard of vigor, they would have gone over every obstacle placed before them... [56]

The above suggestions may have applied when soldiers were encamped and no action was imminent. The recommendations of Surgeon Hewit suggests that maintaining the physical condition of the men superseded any other elements in conducting army operations; that responding to enemy movements was less important; that prolonged forced marches to gain the advantage were secondary.

Had the army commanders in the Gettysburg campaign followed Surgeon Hewit's advice, for example, the battle may have been fought elsewhere. Generals Hooker or Meade had to make up a four-day delay in shadowing the Army of Northern Virginia when it launched the campaign.   The Army of the Potomac had no leisure time for recuperative rest breaks while Lee's unopposed army plundered and destroyed property in Maryland and Pennsylvania.

More often than not, the culmination of battles did not begin with rested soldiers. Campaigns often started with extended or forced marches where armies maneuvered to gain the advantage. They involved re-positioning large bodies of men, artillery, and thousands of vehicles loaded with equipment and supplies. Preparing positions for battle continued to drain men of their fighting strength. This cumulative hyperactivity was the primary cause of soldiers' physical stress. Extreme fatigue was prevalent and could even lead to catatonia.

Commanders, then, had to push their soldiers to their limits and even beyond what most humans consider possible. This was done despite recognition that the physical fighting strength of an army's soldiers was an elementary part of producing a successful outcome. Urgent matters of winning an action or, at least not suffering a defeat, called for desperate decisions and de-emphasizing the need to give troops proper rest. Commanders could worry about the remaining levels of physical strength for fighting at a later time.

Forced Marches

Marches, in themselves, were a difficult test of endurance for the human body. Soldiers were trapped in stifling wool uniforms; they endured the agonizing pain of blistering and bloody feet; they had limited opportunity for rest breaks and breathed the choking atmosphere of dust kicked up by an army in motion.

Artillery, cavalry, and infantry units aggravated each other by their unwillingness to give up the right-of-way. Each branch traveled at a different pace and there was no consistency to uninterrupted motion. The losers followed behind, eating dust and moaning about the insufferable stops and starts caused by the others ahead. [In today's army, it is called an "accordion effect."]

Tall men, especially, proved to be poor material for a long, arduous campaign. While they took longer strides, the shorter men outlasted them. One commented, "When, after a hard, forced march, the captain looked over his company at nightfall to see how many men he had with him, the 'ponies' who trudged along at the tail of the company were generally all there; it was the head end of the company that was thinned out." [57]

Banks' Advance. CEHB/*LICW*

A Confederate soldier, William Watson, listed the reasons on where the best place was to be in line:

> To be on the right of an advancing column, though perhaps attended with a little more danger, has some advantages. In hot dry weather you are out of the crowd, have room for marching, and free from the stifling dust. You also have the first chance of getting clean water from the springs or creeks on the road, before it has been disturbed by the crowd in the crush to obtain it. You have also an opportunity of knowing what is going on by seeing clear in front and being amongst the leading commanders, observing their movements and hearing their conversation. [58]

Gen. Stannard, commanding the Vermont Brigade at Gettysburg, described the harrowing march his men encountered on the way to the battle:

…The Second Vermont Brigade, under my command, marched from the line of the Defenses of Washington, upon the Occoquan, on the 25th ultimo, under orders to report to Major-General Reynolds, commanding the First Army Corps. The brigade joined that corps at this place on the evening of July 1, after an exhausting march of seven days' duration. The distance marched averaged about 18 miles per day. The men marched well, with no straggling. Rain fell on every day of the seven, and considering the condition of the roads, the distance traveled (from the mouth of Occoquan to Gettysburg) could not have been accomplished in less time. [59]

Marching in the rain. EF/*CWAR*

The Federal effort to confront Lee's forces accelerated increasingly in the final few days before the battle of Gettysburg began. The push called for night marches, not unusual during critical circumstances. One soldier in the 20th Maine described his observation of a night march: "The night was full of wanderers and wakers of sleeping men, asking the anxious question that would go on through the nights forever where armies move, 'Hey soldier, what outfit is this?'" [60]

Meade pressed his forces to arrive and meet the enemy for battle:

To Major-General SEDGWICK:

General: The major-general commanding directs me to say that a general battle seems to be impending to-morrow at Gettysburg; that it is of the utmost importance that your command should be up. He directs that you stop all trains that impede your progress, or turn them out of the road. Your march will have to be a forced one to reach the scene of action, where we shall probably be largely outnumbered without your presence.

If any shorter road presents itself, without difficulty in getting up, you will use your discretion in taking it, and report the facts to these headquarters. [61]

Night March EF/LOC

To comply, Gen. Sedwick, in command of the 6th corps, performed a staggering thirty-five mile night/day march with his 13,000 men in only seventeen hours. Fortunately for those tired men, most did not participate in the battle. But for those that did, the fighting strength from these drained warriors was minimal.

On the Confederate side, July 2nd, Law's Alabama brigade marched twenty-six miles in July heat. After a brief rest, it added another mile towards Devil's Den or over the steep incline of Big Round Top to attack Little Round Top five times the same day. They did it without water. In this case the bayonets of the 20th Maine Infantry defeated armed attackers twice its strength. It would be unreasonable to deny that the marathon march robbed the Alabamians of their fighting might and that physical stress was not a factor in their defeat.

Physical fatigue obviously affected soldiers' ability to perform tasks and think. It altered human reactions; it provoked short tempers; it wore down the fighting spirit of units; it altered the ability to reason and promoted poor judgment. In a fatigued state, a unit lost its edge, its alertness, its ability to respond to actions in a logical manner, and its focus on the objective.

Fatigue affected lack of vigilance and cause the defeat or severe punishment of an able, but exhausted, command. For many battles, in retrospect, it is obvious that some plans were not properly conceived, battle lines were not secured because of the lack of caution, verbal orders were not conveyed properly, or important details of communications were misunderstood or forgotten; fatigue, undoubtedly, was a contributing factor.

Fatigue also interfered with the memory process, making it difficult soon after to recollect basic and important details of an action or the correct sequence of them. It helps explain why there are so many irreconcilable assertions of fact regarding the same incidents.

How much did fatigue affect the accuracy of information in after-action reports or eyewitness narratives documenting the event for posterity? The evidence in the accuracy of historic documentation is observable in the wide variety of conflicting accounts. Some deviate so much, it is questionable whether the eyewitnesses were describing the same action.

Enlightenment and increased accuracy describing events occurred later. As Maj. Scheibert of the Prussian Royal Engineers, an eyewitness to the battle of Gettysburg, put it: "[Illumination happened] not immediately after the battle, when personal impressions are conflicting, but after a lapse of more than ten years, when time and matured judgment have ripened the fresh sketch into a splendid picture." [62]

Weather

One of the main factors affecting soldiers' nerves was exposure to weather. It was another stressor which altered soldiers' efficiency. It degraded mental faculties to sort information and perceive situations accurately. Whether in the snow or blazing sun, drenching storms, and steamy humidity, the route of march induced a numbing fatigue. It transformed men into zombie-like figures moving in robotic replication to the pace of the man in front.

Bivouac in the snow. RFZ/*B & L*

Prolonged exposure wore out armies, caused deaths of some, and maimed others permanently. The 148th Pennsylvania of the 1st Corps, for example, suffered an extremely tough march from Falmouth, Virginia to Gettysburg. Although overjoyed at returning to their native state, men left the ranks occasionally, suffering from a number of ailments.

Before the war, one member of the unit, William Mackey, had been a carpenter. During the march he suffered a debilitating sunstroke that caused a condition of nervous prostration and partial paralysis for the rest of his life. He could no longer perform his trade outdoors but, instead, worked at planing doors in a factory. He was also subject to temporary sun blindness.

While not counted in the lengthy lists of those men maimed for life by shot and shell, Mackey and hundreds more, nevertheless, suffered life-altering, permanent health problems from the over-exertions of long marches to and from battlefields.[63]

Fatigue and the "jitters"

In the retreat from Chaffin's Bluff, Va., April, 1865, a Confederate Major described the destructive effects of hard marching:

> ...I preferred to be on foot, for the very purpose of moving around among the men and rousing them when we resumed the march. With this view I was a good part of the time at the rear of the battalion; but notwithstanding my efforts in this respect, individually and through a detail of men selected and organized for the purpose of waking the sleepers, we lost, I am satisfied, every time we resumed the march after a halt at night—men who were not found or who could not be roused.
>
> The nervousness resulting from this constant strain of starvation, fatigue, and lack of sleep was a dangerous thing, at one time producing very lamentable results, which threatened to be even more serious than they were. One evening an officer, I think of one of our supply departments, passed and re-passed us several times, riding a powerful black stallion, all of whose furnishings—girths, reins, etc.,—were very heavy, indicating the unmanageable character of the horse. When he rode ahead the last time, about dark, it seems that he imprudently hitched his horse by tying his very stout tie rein to a heavy fence rail which was part of the road fence.
>
> Something frightened the animal and he reared back, pulling the rail out of the fence and dragging it after him full gallop down the road crowded with troops, mowing them down like the scythe of a war chariot. Someone, thinking there was a charge of cavalry, fired his musket and, on the instant, three or four battalions, mine among them, began firing into each other.
>
> I was never more alarmed. Muskets were discharged in my very face, and I fully expected to be shot down but after the most trying and perilous experience, the commanding officers succeeded in getting control of their men and getting them again into formation. But while we were talking to them, suddenly the panic seized them again, and they rushed in such a wild rout against the heavy road fence that they swept it away, and many of them took to the woods, firing back as they ran.
>
> A second time the excitement was quieted and a third time it broke out. By this time, however, I had fully explained to my men that we had just

put out fresh flankers on both sides of the road, that we could not have an attack of cavalry without warning from them, and that the safe and soldierly thing to do was to lie down until everything should become calm. I was much pleased that this third time my command did not fire a shot, while the battalions in our front and rear were firing heavily. A field officer and a good many other officers and men were killed and wounded in these alarms, just how many I do not believe was ever ascertained. [64]

Effects of Forced Marches as Evidenced by Animal Losses

From the Gettysburg campaign report of Capt. E. B. Brunson, C. S. Artillery, commanding Reserve Artillery Battalion:

No incident worthy of notice occurred on the march to this place, and I may say it was most successfully conducted, especially when we consider the miserable condition of the horses' feet, for lack of shoes, on the limestone pikes, over which a large portion of our march was made. My ordnance officer made every effort to obtain shoes, as did the chief of artillery, so I am informed, but without avail. Consequently, we were obliged to abandon some 20 horses by the time we reached this encampment. [65]

Listed below is the number of public animals belonging to the 11th Corps, Army of Potomac, which had been lost, killed, or abandoned on the route of march since June 12, 1863.

Horses abandoned from exhaustion	55
Horses abandoned from lameness	16
Horses abandoned from glanders	3
Horses captured by enemy	13
Horses strayed or stolen	7
Horses died on the march	15
Horses killed in battle	98
Mules abandoned from exhaustion	12
Mules abandoned from lameness	3
Mules drowned in the Potomac	2
Mules captured by the enemy	26
Mules strayed or stolen	2
Mules died on the march	7
Total	259 [66]

From this report, it is noteworthy that almost as many horses died from exhaustion, lameness, or on the march as those killed in battle. Note also that no mules were killed in battle. Easily spooked by loud noise and unmanageable in battle, they didn't pull artillery pieces. While there are many Civil War photographs showing horses killed in battle, there are few with dead mules.

According to Lt. Col. William Le Duc, Chief Quartermaster, 11th Corps, many of the animal losses were preventable. He wrote:

> ...Fifty-five horses were abandoned from exhaustion. Of these, 45 were artillery horses [the average life span of an artillery horse was 7 ½ months]. Artillery horses are not under control of the quartermaster's department after being transferred to the batteries. But it is well known that artillery is the most destructive branch of service upon horses, and although not exactly pertinent to this report, I will venture the suggestion that the cause is mostly in the very faulty and unnecessarily bad method of hitching the horses to the load. The weight of the guns or caissons is not sufficient to account for the bad condition of the animals. I believe four horses properly hitched will do the work now expected of six, and keep in good order, if hitched so as properly and fairly to divide the labor and equalize the draft upon the shoulders of the animals. In fact, I have reason to know from actual experiment that the hitching and harnessing of artillery horses has much if not most to do with the rapid deterioration of the animals. [67]

Advancing under difficulties. WT/*B & L*

Sleep Deprivation

Impairment of Ability

Hard marching, fighting, or digging in was often accompanied by the great nullifier of an army's strengths and wits—sleep deprivation. It turned capable soldiers into helpless ones. It made alert minds dull, strong men weak, and sapped the will to fight.

Jeb Stuart's Confederate cavalrymen, for example, accomplished a remarkable journey in their long ride to Gettysburg around the Army of the Potomac. But it was not without a price. Stuart's horse soldiers spent thirty-six hours in the saddle, interrupted by their fight at the battle of Hanover on June 30th. This was followed by an all-night march to Carlisle, Pennsylvania in search of the main body of Lee's army. General Stuart described the trek and the state of mind borne by his tired soldiers as they approached Gettysburg:

> The night's march over a very dark road was one of peculiar hardship, owing to loss of rest to both man and horse. After a series of exciting combats and night marches, it was a severe tax to their endurance. Whole regiments slept in the saddle, their faithful animals keeping the road unguided. In some instances they fell from their horses, overcome with physical fatigue and sleepiness. [68]

One cavalryman described the condition of his men:

> It is impossible for me to give you a correct idea of the fatigue and exhaustion of our men and beasts at this time. From our great exertion, constant mental excitement, want of sleep and food, the men were overcome and so tired and stupid as almost to be ignorant of what was taking place around them. Couriers in attempting to deliver orders to officers would be compelled to give them a shake and call before they could make them understand. [69]

The effects from the lack of sleep are numerous. They include: irritability, blurred vision, impaired motor skills, slurred speech, memory lapses or memory loss, overall confusion, hallucinations, nausea, anxiety, psychosis, depression, decreased mental activity, decreased concentration, impatience, slowed reaction time, misbehavior, hypertension or hyperactivity, increased blood pressure, dizziness, aching muscles, and degradation of the immune system to fight off sickness or infection.

The toxic concoction of sleep deprivation, hard marching, exertions of combat and adrenaline rushes caused unpredictable conduct in men, producing "uncharacteristic behavior patterns from deep gloom to wild elation." [70]

Confederate Major Robert Stiles compared his view of sleep deprivation versus food deprivation when he commented on Mr. George Cary Eggleston's paper describing the pains and pangs of hunger, and how deeply they depressed and deteriorated his entire being during the campaign of '64:

> I take no issue with him as to this statement, and yet, to me, even greater suffering and deterioration came from lack of sleep. I do not know that I have ever suffered more, physically and mentally, than from intense desire and demand of my whole being for deep, unbroken sleep, combined with inability to get more than a snatch at a time, which was almost worse than none at all. Such was frequently our experience, especially upon night marches and during long-continued battle.
>
> I am inclined to think my unusual muscular strength saved me from that general giving way which, in the case of most men, follows quickly upon lack of sufficient food; but on the other hand, I seemed to be peculiarly susceptible to the suffering, even torture and almost madness, which accompanies or follows lack of sleep. [71]

The night in the apple orchard. JFQ/*CWAR*

The unavoidable urge for sleep was the natural occurrence of the body to recuperate and repair itself for the next exertions. For some, a deep sleep in a tranquil setting produced an amazing recovery in very short time. Col. E.P. Alexander, Confederate artilleryman, reflected on the recuperative effects of sleep when at Chancellorsville:

> In ten seconds I was...sounder asleep than I had ever been before, or ever realized that it was possible to be. For there is a sort of higher power of sleep, with qualities as entirely different from the ordinary as light is from heat. I don't think that mere fatigue, or loss of ordinary sleep, produces this higher power of sleep, because I have never been able to obtain it except in connection with the excitement attendant on a battle & not more than three or four times even then.
>
> This was my first experience of it & the recollection of no pleasure of all my life is more vivid & enduring than that of this letting myself, as it were, sink under a dense fluid which penetrated alike eyes & ears & pores until it pervaded the very bones bringing with it, instantly, everywhere a trance of delicious rest & freedom even from dreams. It does not seem possible to dream, but yet the oblivion is half conscious.
>
> Could death ever come as that sleep did it would be delicious to die. [Colonel Lindsey] Walker was not gone ten minutes but when he waked me I came back from a long ways. But I came easily & felt at once refreshed wonderfully, as if by a strong cordial. [72]

Officers at all command levels were the ones who suffered sleep deprivation more than any others. Yet, they were the ones expected to make logical decisions and exercise sound judgment. It was their minds, not muscles, which were to make the most valuable contributions. They were the ones that needed sleep the most.

Night council WLS/*B & L*

As troops rested, it was they who caused the army to function. Lower grade officers kept track of their men, maintained personnel records, and prepared reports to supply their commands. High-ranking officers attended nighttime planning councils. They crafted itineraries, laid out the orders of march for the following day, arranged rendezvous points and river crossings, issued and reviewed orders, and formulated plans. Strategy meetings required an unimpaired mental ability, attention to detail, clear-minded assessment of situations, and, in the process, an attempt to outthink the enemy.

Gen. Patton, of World War II fame once said that "tired officers are always pessimists." Skepticism may well have undermined workable plans, endangered troops, and contributed to defeat. The fate of many a soldier wrested in the belief that commanders' judgments were made with qualified deliberation and consideration for the well-being of the men. Studies have shown, however, that a total loss of sleep causes people to take unnecessary risks, that total sleep deprivation for one night produced many errors and after the second night, the errors were significant. [73]

Night combat was an especially difficult challenge. It aggravated the soldiers' level of fatigue more than daytime combat. It not only curtailed sleep, but also intruded upon the body's mechanism, the diurnal cycle, that affected the soldiers' physiological functions. Humans are at their best performance between noon and 9 p.m. They are the least efficient between 11 p.m. and 6 a.m. [74]

Night fighting was not the norm, but it did occur and was dangerous. It was hard to distinguish shadowy figures and impossible to see the colors of uniforms. Aiming weapons focused on sounds made by suspected enemy troops or the blaze of muskets rather than attempting to discern vague impressions of figures in the night. Casualties from "friendly fire" were not uncommon.

Friendly fire killed and wounded a number of soldiers at Gettysburg. On Culp's Hill, July 2, Col. Abel Godard, 60th N.Y., Green's Brigade, reported the difficulties in night-fighting: "The darkness was so great in this part of the woods that we could not see the enemy, and we fired at the flashes of their guns." He further stated: "I regret to have to report that a portion of the line in the trenches commenced firing before our skirmishers had come in, killing and wounding several." [75]

Extreme Fatigue

Extreme fatigue was the end result of the body responding to several reactions: first, the high consumption of human energy used in getting to the battlefield, second, fighting in the battle, and third, the overcharges of adrenaline the body called upon to meet the energy requirements produced from physical activity and excitement.

For some soldiers, extreme fatigue, protracted and taken a step further, leads ultimately to their psychiatric breakdown in battle. Psychologist F. C. Bartlett wrote, "In war there is perhaps no general condition which is more likely to produce a large crop of nervous and mental disorders than a state of prolonged and great fatigue." [76]

It was two o'clock in the morning at Gettysburg, July 2nd, when Gen. Meade learned that two of his corps had been disastrously defeated and 10,000 men of the rank and file in his army were wiped from the rolls. He also discovered that:

> ...one of the best of his corps commanders, Gen. Reynolds, on whom he had relied upon with the greatest confidence, had been killed...As yet unaccustomed to handling and disposing of a large army, and diffident of his own powers and capacity to do so, it is no wonder that he did not at

that time prove himself as equal to the exigencies of the occasion as he so successfully did at subsequent periods of his command of that army. Gen. Doubleday, who saw him that morning, says: "When I saw him soon after daylight he seemed utterly worn out and hollow-eyed. Anxiety and want of sleep were evidently telling upon him." [77]

Exertions from Combat

While adrenalin supplied the extra strength needed for the body to operate during stimulating circumstances, the inevitable reaction would be total exhaustion or near-collapse. Allen C. Redwood, 55th Va., gave his impression of what the physical effects were like after combat: "Think you of a gang of coal-heavers who have just finished putting in a winter's supply ordered by some provident householder in midsummer, and you get a fair impression of troops at the end of a day's fighting." [78]

During the battle of Gettysburg Union forces spent practically the entire battle in a state of motion. Hardly a unit remained in a stationary position. Units either retreated from their original position, advanced from their assigned position, or were sent to reinforce or support other parts of the line. General Meade stated:

> The length of time required to carry and execute the orders...was probably due to the fact that the brigades of the various corps had become more or less separated and the men had become utterly worn out and exhausted...
>
> This separation of the brigades was due to the numerous movements of the troops during the battle. Many of the troops had been moved from one part of the line to another, having been put in action in two different parts of the line the same day. [79]

Stress from combat exertions was particularly heightened for troops on the attack. Attackers abandoned the protection of their positions and moved towards their foe, exposing themselves to the firepower of an enemy, more than likely, well concealed and protected from gunfire. Additionally, attackers often crossed unfamiliar terrain. They had to deal with unforeseen accidents of the ground such as ravines, creeks, obstacles that forced a breakup of connectivity in the formation, and guard against any points of surprise held by the waiting enemy.

In the process, men were exposed to the unsettling effects of viewing their own wounded and dead, the gradual disintegration of their unit's manpower and fighting spirit, and the loss of cohesion that existed when they first stepped off. In addition, the spiritual boost gained from artillery support diminished rapidly when the attack was well underway. Gun crews resorted to firing only the less deadly solid rounds as faulty explosive projectiles frequently detonated among friendly troops in front. Support stopped completely as the attackers closed on the enemy.

The defenders, on the other hand, enjoyed the benefits that so aggravated the attackers. They consumed little or no physical energy in their static positions; they experienced fewer casualties from protected defense works; they had the benefit of using artillery defensively, which was more lethal in that it could use any ammunition they chose, including the most destructive form of close-range ammunition—canister; with better stability maintained by defending formations, they maintained their unity and fighting spirit longer; it was physically easier to fire and hit targets from stationary positions; the defending troops knew the nuances of the ground they occupied; defenders were accessible to reserve supplies of men and ammunition.

Gen. Helmuth von Moltke, the Prussian chief-of-staff, summed up the defenders' superiority over attackers: "It is absolutely beyond doubt that the man who shoots without stirring has the advantage of him who fires while advancing, that the one finds protection in the ground, whereas in it, the other finds obstacles..." [80]

Physical Deprivations

The most important part of a soldier's uniform, the article that wore out the most, the supply item that seemed in perpetual shortage was footwear. Shortages of shoes have always plagued armies on the move. Practically every campaign describes the suffering from the lack of footwear and the repercussions on a force's effectiveness. Marching with injured feet inflicted extreme pain, adding to the exhaustive state of marching men. It reduced a force's manpower by increasing straggling.

Maj. Gen. R. E. Rodes, C.S.A. division commander, noted the condition of his men on the way to Gettysburg:

> Three brigades (Ramseur's, Iverson's, and Doles'), with three batteries of artillery, were ordered across the Potomac at once. It was not until this day that the troops began to exhibit unmistakable signs of exhaustion, and that stragglers could be found in the line of march, and even then none but absolutely worn-out men fell out of line.
>
> The whole march from Culpeper Court-House to Williamsport, which was an extremely rapid one, was executed in a manner highly creditable to the officers and men of the division. A halt at Williamsport was absolutely necessary from the condition of the feet of the unshod men. Very many of these gallant fellows were still marching in ranks, with feet bruised, bleeding, and swollen, and withal so cheerfully as to entitle them to be called the heroes of the Pennsylvania campaign. None but the best of soldiers could have made such a march under such circumstances.
> [81]

Shoe problems are attributed almost exclusively to the Confederate army. The Union army, however, suffered as well. On the march to Gettysburg, it was rapidly trying to catch up with Lee's four-day head start. Supply depots that could supply footwear were re-positioning and inaccessible.

The itineraries and pace of advance on either side substantiate the punishing wear and tear on shoes. Even modern-day versions would not take the punishment of such grueling, frequent marathons. Marches of 15 to 25 miles a day were done repeatedly. Shoe leather was soaked in rains or, in some cases, men were not allowed to remove footwear when fording streams. Constant exposure of footwear to wet and dry conditions combined with punishing marches over rough roads disintegrated leather and the threads binding shoes together, leaving thousands to face the agony of the march.

This significant item, however, critical to army movement, didn't seem to figure a great deal into the planning process of such important undertakings. To launch a major operation, commanders spent months gathering manpower, re-assigning units, re-designing the army structure, gathering equipment and

Confederates at a ford. ACR/*B & L*

supplies, yet it is apparent that there never seemed to be enough shoes. Commanders certainly knew the risk and consequences of a shoeless fighting force.

It is difficult to name an operation that ran out of ammunition. Shoe shortages, however, seemed without remedy. Perhaps subsisting off those killed on the battlefield was the expected source of supply.

Shoeless dead at Gettysburg
WT [From a Gardner photo]/*B & L*

Just before Gettysburg, June 28, Rufus Ingalls, Brig. Gen., and Chief Quartermaster, Army of the Potomac, requested an emergency shipment of footwear from Gen. Meigs, Quartermaster-General, Washington: "After the late long marches in wet weather, many shoes will be needed. Will you please order forward at once 10,000 pairs of bootees and same number of socks, for issue as the corps pass here?" [82]

Just after Gettysburg, July 8, Maj. Gen. Howard, Union 11th Corps commander, described the reduced condition of his force for lack of footwear:

(Care of Brigadier-General Ingalls, chief quartermaster, Army of the Potomac, Frederick, Md.) One-half of the effective strength of the corps cannot march for want of shoes and stockings, and will be left here, under a proper commander. Draw 3,000 pairs of shoes and 5,000 pairs of stockings at once from General Ingalls, and forward them to this place. The remainder of the corps moves as soon as provisions arrive.

You will use your utmost endeavors to render the corps effective again by refitting the same. Answer. [83]

Food Deprivation

Food deprivation was another key element in spelling disaster for an army. It not only weakened men, it disheartened them and fixated their attention on satisfying their hunger. While the emotion of self preservation was ever-present, the urge to replenish famished stomachs, even in combat, sometimes competed with the will to survive.

At Gettysburg, July 2nd, as Kershaw's Brigade advanced towards the Rose Farm, a company of the 14th South Carolina Volunteers was sent forward as skirmishers. In crossing a field toward the enemy, they ran into a large patch of ripe blackberries. They paused to pick and eat the delicious bounty, all the while moving slowly towards the enemy. This pleasant distraction didn't return to reality until the men had closed within 50 yards of the enemy's advanced line. With a Rebel yell, the men sprang forward and back to the business at hand. [84]

Also at Gettysburg on July 2nd, Confederate infantry overran Federal guns on East Cemetery Hill; while many of the Union infantrymen retreated to the rear, the gutsy Union artillerymen of Stewart's battery, who lined the Baltimore Pike, held up fence rails to stop the runaways; gutsier still, Stewart's men robbed food from the retreating men in the midst of the struggle to save the hill. [85]

Food deprivation handicapped fighting ability. Confederate Major Robert Stiles commented on a condition caused by the lack of proper food rations in the Army of Northern Virginia:

> Perhaps the most peculiar and striking fact or feature of the physical condition of General Lee's army during the latter half of the war was night blindness—the men affected being unable to see after sunset, or a little later.
>
> I do not know what proportion of the men were so affected, but it is safe to say that thousands were. Many of them were as good and true men as any in the service; indeed, I have seen men led by the hand all night in order to go into battle with the command in the morning.
>
> The doctors tell us that these symptoms were to be accounted for as among the expressions of an anaemic [sic] and scorbutic condition, which condition resulted from lack of proper and sufficient nutrition. [86]

Stress from Observations of the Senses:

This difficulty of seeing things correctly…makes things appear quite different to what was expected. The impression of the senses is stronger than the force of the ideas resulting from methodical reflection, and this goes so far that no important undertaking was ever yet carried out without the Commander having to subdue new doubts in himself at the time of commencing the execution of his work. Von Clausewitz [87]

Many veterans maintained a vivid sensory recollection of their combat experiences—memories that lasted a lifetime. They remembered the sounds, the sights, the smells, and the tastes. Some even recalled their sense of touch. One modern-day veteran said he remembered "the wet, sticky sensation when I touched one of my wounded soldiers one last time before the medevac rushed him forever from our presence..." [88]

Aural Stressors

Exposure to noise related to stress, in early general research, was termed as an "annoyance." Further research, however, indicated that high levels of noise produced a multitude of psychological and behavioral effects. Civil War soldiers, especially, had no shortage of opportunities for exposure to the physically damaging and mentally harmful sounds of battle.

Aural exposure to combat included many varieties. Each had their unforgettable signature sounds: the frightening near-miss zip of bullets smashing into rock, wood or vegetation, the thud of lead piercing flesh, or the snapping sound of projectiles shattering bones of man and beast. On a larger scale there were detonations of thousands of muskets from massed infantry, not so much distinguishable as rapid single discharges but more like a constant, inescapable roar. And finally, there was the god of all battle sounds—the earthshaking, deafening roar of artillery. [89]

Artillery fire was the chief cause of aural stress. Men who were positioned near or among their gun batteries were exposed to the maximum noise levels that battles could generate. During the Atlanta campaign of 1864, H. Earnest Goodman, U.S. Army Surgeon in Chief, reported that "the shelling caused the death of one man from fright." [90]

First Lt. L. A. Smith, 136th New York Infantry, recollected the discomfort created in his unit from nearby friendly batteries during the July 3rd cannonade:

> It is a terrible experience to support batteries when located in their front...I don't believe men ever suffered more in the same time than those who lay along the [Taneytown] road in front of the cemetery on that memorable day...In spite of all a soldier's ingenuity in adjusting himself to the situation there was no relief; the last condition was always worse than the preceding. If you laid down on the ground and put your fingers in your ears you got, in addition to the crash in the air, the full effect of the earth's tremor and its additional force as a conductor.
>
> One of our men found afterwards that his teeth were loose and within a few days nearly all of them dropped out...If you rolled over on your

back and looked up into the heavens fairly black with missiles exploding continually and sending their broken fragments in every direction, the situation was not more assuring.

If you sat down with your back to the stone wall and looked over into the cemetery, you saw long fiery tongues leaping toward you, thick clouds of sulphurous smoke settle down around you, blackening the countenance almost beyond recognition.

If you turned around and looked over the wall toward the enemy, each cannon ball seemed directed toward that particular spot. [91]

Commanders were well aware of the psychological value of artillery and used its sound to create or intensify the enemy's lack of confidence and sap the will to fight. One soldier described the sound of artillery shells: "These missiles howled like demons, and made us cower in the smallest possible space, and wish we had each a little red cap in the fairy tale, which, by putting on our heads, would make us invisible." [92]

Explosive projectiles were even more stressful. First, there was the release of the explosion from the propellant charge. This was followed by the sound of the fragmenting charge in the shell, producing an unsettling effect on men and horses, not only from the burst, but from the bright flashes of energy released.

The sound of friendly musket fire could also unravel a steadfast battle line. At Fredericksburg, December, 1862, Union Brig. Gen Nelson Taylor, commanding 3rd Brigade, reported:

> Finding the right of my line exposed to two or three of the enemy's guns, using grape and canister, I ordered the Eighty-eighth Regiment forward under the cover of a slight elevation of ground, with directions to fire a volley at the battery.
>
> This was executed, and had the desired effect. The pieces were silenced and immediately withdrew, but, most singular to say, apparently frightened at the noise they had made themselves, with a few exceptions the whole regiment turned and ran toward the rear.
>
> With the assistance of my aide-de-camp, Lieutenant Post, and an intervening ditch, I succeeded in stopping this disgraceful and causeless retrograde movement, and getting the regiment back upon the brigade line again, where it remained during the rest of the engagement, and fully retrieved itself by its firmness and steadiness thereafter. [93]

Aural stress also includes cries from the suffering. At Gettysburg, Union 1st Lt. Frank A. Haskell, aide-de-camp to Brigadier General Gibbon, described the plight of the casualties caught in the bedlam at the Angle during Pickett's Charge: "The frequent dead and wounded lie where they stagger and fall—there is no humanity for them now, none can be spared to care for them. The men do not cheer or shout; they growl and over that uneasy sea, heard with the roar of musketry, sweeps the muttered thunder of a storm of growls." [94]

Shortly afterwards, an officer in the 136th New York Infantry was assigned to picket duty on evening of July 3rd near the Union center. He described the sounds of men across the fields succumbing to the ebbing fever of life:

> The wails of the dying, the prayers and curses of the wounded, the agonizing cries everywhere for "Water, water For God's sake, give me water!" The call of the comrades by name, the frequent call for mother from men, often of mature years, who in the delirium of pain were carried back to their childhood days, all contributed to make it a night never to be forgotten. Toward morning, as the field became more quiet, the call by comrades for missing friends was incessant. The call started where the line of battle commenced, coming nearer and nearer, then past to our left and back again, becoming more and more plaintive and intense as hopes gave way to despair in the unsuccessful search. [95]

Visual Stressors

Joseph Kirkland, 12th Ill. Inf., in his novel *The Captain of Company "K"*, asks the reader:

> How do men fall in battle? Forward, as fall other slaughtered animals…. As they fall, so they lie, so they die and so they stiffen; and all the contortions seen by burial details…are the natural result of the removal of bodies which have fallen with faces and limbs to the earth, and grown rigid without the rearrangement of "decent burial." [96]

Viewing the harm inflicted on other humans during war leaves an indelible impression on the minds of most. From the Civil War, unforgettable memories were branded forever by the constant exposure to scenes of war's destruction— seeing the endless slaughter or mutilation of soldiers, friend or foe.

It was particularly stressful to soldiers who saw their comrades-in-arms, some of them relatives or childhood chums, fall in battle. Soldiers, placed in the midst of an action, were exposed to many such emotional incidents. When these shocks were condensed into one brief period, the results were unbearable.

What did they see? What part of the body received most of the injuries? What caused the most common types of injuries? Studies and calculations were performed involving the frequency in types of wounds, treatments, recovery rates, etc. Specimens were collected for further study in Washington, D.C. [One such specimen from Gettysburg included the famous amputated leg bone of Union Maj. General Daniel Sickles.] The following is from the *Consolidated Classified Statement of Wounds, &c., of the Army of the Potomac, for the period from May 1 to July 31, 1864*:

Location of injury, &c.	Total.
Head and face	3,813
Neck	692
Shoulder	2,145
Thorax	2,527
Abdomen	1,446
Back and hips	3,222
Perineum and genitals	216
Superior extremities	11,110
Inferior extremities	12,203
Large arteries and nerves	34
Total	**36,508**

Deaths in field hospitals	1,272
Shell wounds	2,664
Cannon-shot wounds	121
Bullet wounds	33,292
Bayonet wounds	37
Sword wounds	18
Amputations in field hospitals	2,875
Excisions in field hospitals	568

Average aggregate strength present. 96,294

Medical officers present	561
Killed (by regimental reports)	7,542
Wounded (by regimental reports)	41,946
Missing (by regimental reports)	14,163
Officers wounded	1,902 [97]

Damaging wounds in the Civil War were so severe or treatment of them was so inadequate that no more than half the wounded could be expected to return to the army. For the other half, many would die under the limited medical treatment of the day. Capt. W. H. Bennett, 25th Wisconsin, Co. B, was listed as "wounded and prisoner, July 22, 1864; leg amputated three times; died August 10, 1864 at Macon, Ga., of wounds." Many that did survive, including thousands of amputees, would be forever crippled. [98]

In war, death and injury surround soldiers—from mild wounds to the horrific, from both battle and non-combat situations. Most happened in the ways expected from war. Lt. Wm. J. Rabb, 10th New York Cavalry, Co. D, for example, was "killed at Brandy Station, by a sabre-thrust through the body while lying under his horse; he would not surrender"... Jefferson Coates, 7th Wisconsin, Co. H, was "wounded at South Mountain and Gettysburg; loss of both eyes; brevetted Captain, with medal of honor for gallantry at Gettysburg." [99]

Beyond injuries from bullets and artillery shells, however, some were unique:

- During the retreat through Gettysburg on July 1st, Capt. John E. Cook, 76th N.Y. reported how some of his men's casualties were sustained: "Being out of ammunition, the 94th N. Y. relieved us, and we were not again under fire until we passed through Gettysburg. Here we lost 8 or 10 men by *falling bricks* and infantry fire in the streets...." [100]

- Lt. Col. William H. Moody, commanding the 139th Pa. Volunteers, reported: "[At Gettysburg] early on the morning of the 3rd, Col. F. H. Collier [then commanding] accidentally shot himself through the foot with a pistol-ball, and was compelled to leave his command." [101]

- During the July 3rd cannonade, one of the color guards in the 136th N. Y. Infantry "had a fragment of a rock driven into his head, causing instant death." [102]

- General Hancock, mounted on his horse during Pickett's Charge, was severely wounded by a bullet and a "ten penny weight iron nail, bent double." It was theorized that the nail was used in the construction of his saddle and was driven into him along with the bullet. Saddlers, however, said that a nail of such size was not used in saddle-making and speculated that it was fired from a gun. [103]

- 112th Illinois, Co. A:—Lorenzo Brown; kicked to death by a mule at Somerset, Ky., April 23, 1864.

- 56th New York, Co. F:—John Hoffman; killed by lightning at Cashtown, Maryland.

- 11th Vermont, Co. B:—Lt. Edward B. Parker; died a prisoner at Columbia, S.C., Oct. 13, 1864, from injuries received from bloodhounds.

- 4th New Jersey, Co. C:—Geo. W. Hindley; died in a fit at Alexandria, Va., Oct. 7, 1861.

- 5th New York Cavalry, Co. H:—Lt. J. A. Benedict; died from amputation of right arm resulting from the bite of a man on thumb, Dec. 11, 1861.

- 52nd Indiana, Co. B:—Timothy Westport; discharged April 27, 1863, for loss of speech.

- 8th New York, Co. A:—A. Lohman; died of poison while on picket, by drinking from a bottle found at a deserted house. [104]

While this work is not intended to dwell on the horrific, the point of what men saw cannot be accurately conveyed without some examples: At Winchester, June, 1863, Confederate Artillery Maj. Robert Stiles described "a scene of horror and of agony so extreme that I would not describe it, were it not that a knowledge of the widest swings of the pendulum of war, through the entire orbit of human experiences and emotions, is needed for adequate appreciation of the life of the soldier:"

> The entire battalion, Hilary Jones', was moving in column, the Charlottesville battery, in which I was serving, following immediately after Garber's. The farm road we were using led between two heavy old-fashioned crate posts. My recollection is that they were of stone and that there was no gate and no fence on either side of the posts, but the ground outside of and near the posts was somewhat rough and steep. One of Garber's men, belonging to his rear gun, attempted to run abreast of the piece between the gate posts, presumably to avoid the rough ground outside. There was not room enough for him to pass, and the wheel crowding him against the post, the washer hook caught and tore open his abdomen, dragging the poor wretch along by his intestines, which were literally pulled from his body in a long, gory ribbon. [105]

There were other visual stressors besides witnessing mutilating injuries. Viewing the actions of some could spark chain reactions from others. Just a handful of troops, for example, in a heightened state of stress, could ruin the shock effect of their line's firepower by a prematurely burst of fire and provoke gunfire down the entire battle line. Seeing soldiers giving way down the line could trigger a feeling of isolation. Even a scene of just a few men running to the rear for safety could induce a stampede by stressed troops that remained. A view of a forward skirmish line, melting back to the rear to act as supports was inevitable in battle; the scene of men "retreating," nevertheless, could be unnerving.

Reaction from stress was more pronounced in formations that were dispersed. A dispersed skirmish line, for example, did not have the connectivity inherent in the compact battle lines of regiments, held together by shoulder-to-shoulder contact.

But even regimental formations could be unnerved. This was especially true if lines of units were not totally visible to its members. A deployed line, for example, made invisible by terrain features gave soldiers the false impression of isolation from the main body. [106]

The "fog of war" was a major stressor. Rapid actions forced commanders to make quick decisions sometimes based on misperception of the enemy's intentions. At Gettysburg on July 1st, for example, Confederate Gen. Robert Rodes, division commander, perceived that an enemy division, under Gen. Robinson, was extending the Union line on Oak Ridge to assault his men.

"Finding that the enemy was rash enough to come out from the woods to attack me," Rodes stated, "I determined to meet him when he got to the foot of the hill I occupied..."   Robinson was, in fact, merely making a defensive move by extending his line to protect the Union right flank. [107]

Sometimes the "fog of war" caused misperception of actions among friendly troops. The 151st Pa. of Biddle's Brigade on July 1st was ordered forward to McPherson's Ridge to fill in a gap in the line of battle on its immediate front. The adjacent unit it was supposed to connect with "evidently considered the 151st Pa...a relief; and immediately fell back to the hollow and reformed, thus exposing the right of the 151st. The great loss of the 151st regiment occurred at this time..." [108]

Smells

Soldiers sometimes describe the odor of battle as unforgettable. While it seems easier to recollect an image of a place or person, or the sound of musical notes from the past, the smell of death, blood, and smoke also produced a memorable concoction that lasted a lifetime.

At Gettysburg, for example, 7,000 soldiers were killed outright. Up to 5,000 horses and mules were slain. The combined weight of this death mass of remains fermenting in the blazing July sun amounted to 8 ½ million pounds. Soldiers vomited just from the stench. Locals wore camphor under their noses or cologne to mask the odor. Reports said that the odor could be detected in Harrisburg, Pennsylvania, forty miles away.

Lt. L. A. Smith, in surveying the ground near the Union center on July 4th commented that "the slaughter here had been fearful, and the stench was sickening. The dead were swollen until their strained and torn clothing could hardly contain their bodies; some were very giants in size." [109]

Confederate Maj. Robert Stiles described the scene of horror "to give to those who have had no actual experience of war some approximate conception of the variety and extravagance of horrors which the soldier is called upon, from time to time, to undergo:"

> On the 4th of July, in readjusting and straightening our lines, the guns of Hilary Jones' battalion were put in position, on a part of the field which Hill's corps had fought over on the 1st and upon which the pioneer corps and burying parties had not been able to complete their work; so that the dead bodies of men and horses had lain there putrefying under the summer sun for three days.
>
> The sights and smells that assailed us were simply indescribable— corpses swollen to twice their original size, some of them actually burst asunder with the pressure of foul gases and vapors. I recall one feature never before noted, the shocking distension and protrusion of the eyeballs of dead men and dead horses.

Dead at the Stone wall near Marye's Heights WT/*B & L*

Several human or unhuman [sic] corpses sat upright against a fence, with arms extended in the air and faces hideous with something very like a fixed leer, as if taking a fiendish pleasure in showing us what we essentially were and might at any moment become.

The odors were nauseating, and so deadly that in a short time we all sickened and were lying with our mouths close to the ground, most of us vomiting profusely. We protested against the cruelty and folly of keeping men in such a position.

Of course to fight in it was utterly out of the question, and we were soon moved away; but, for the rest of that day and late into the night, the fearful odors I had inhaled remained with me and made me loathe myself as if an already rotting corpse. [110]

At the battle of Cold Harbor, June, 1864, Maj. Stiles again commented on the stench of battle: "There was a good deal of smoke in the air from the woods afire out in front, and we soon became conscious of an insufferable odor of burning flesh… The colonel told us, too, what we already suspected, that the odor which so offended our nostrils was that of human bodies roasting in the forest fires in front." [111]

Mental Stress

The first half of the war consisted of sporadic periods of relative peace, sometimes lasting for months, mixed with several battles lasting from one to

Rescuing wounded from burning woods. EF/*B & L*

three days. In 1863, the Army of the Potomac fought only five days of heavy combat.

When a major battle was fought, each army rested, replaced its losses, fought another battle, rested, and rebuilt again. Little was happening to end the war. During quiet periods, men spent months trapped in the tedium of camp life. Their main fight was simply to overcome boredom and the monotony of routines that never seemed to change. They drilled day in and day out.

Mental stress occurred long before battles began. It was activated when armies switched from the accustomed comfortable lifestyle and tranquil tedium of encampment to a mobile situation fraught with danger, uncertainty, and the prolonged strain of physical activity. It started with a sudden and rushed increase in preparatory activities and accompanied with the excitement that broke the boredom. It climaxed when soldiers were catapulted into a situation swirling with shock and terror. The transition was surely stressful, both physically and mentally.

Conflicts of Values

Soldiers in any era, from any nation, are confronted with a series of predicaments that force them to betray personal feelings for principles that are deemed more important—a conflict of values.

Respecting life, for example, is a universal principle of mankind. "Thou shalt not kill!" This code is held by most cultures and religions. The thought of killing another human being is repugnant to most. As soldiers, it bothered some more than others. The act of killing another human, even for a noble reason, was certainly a mental stressor and caused permanent anguish.

Conflicts of values could trigger profound mental stress in resolving deeply held beliefs. A study from World War II listed the stressors caused by such clashes within oneself:

- Between requirements of duty and impulse to safety and comfort
- Between duty and obligation to family to whose well-being the soldiers survival is important
- Between informal group codes as of loyalty to comrades and formal requirements of the military situation which may not permit mutual aid
- Between previously accepted moral codes and combat imperatives
- Being treated as a means rather than an end in oneself
- Seemingly arbitrary and impersonal demands of coercive authority
- Sense of not counting as an individual [112]

Civilians, generally, are not confronted with such weighty issues, at least not all at the same time. Soldiers, on the other hand had to deal with each one and do it simultaneously.

Furthermore, little attention has been given to the mental plight of soldiers who worried about the welfare of their families back home. Many dependents relied on their absent soldier-providers to continue to care for their well-being as responsible husbands, sons, and fathers. For many, it was the greatest conflict of values between their duty as soldiers and obligations to family.

An officer in the Army of Northern Virginia described the mental burden placed on those performing their duty:

...It is my deliberate conviction that Southern soldiers who remained faithful under the unspeakable pressure of letters and messages revealing suffering, starvation, and despair at home, displayed a heroism and devotion well-nigh superhuman.

The men who felt this strain most were husbands of young wives and fathers of young children, whom they had supported by their labor, manual or mental. As the lines of communication in the Confederacy were more and more broken and destroyed, and the ability, both of county and public authorities and of neighbors, to aid them became less and less—the situation of such families became more and more desperate, and their appeals more and more piteous to their only earthly helpers who were far away, filling their places in "the thin gray line."

...Ask any Confederate officer who commanded troops during the latter part of the war and who was loved and trusted by his men. He will tell you of letters which it would have seared your very eyeballs to read, but that they could not be read without tears—letters in which a wife and mother, crazed by her starving children's cries for bread, required a husband and father to choose between his God-imposed obligations to her and to them and his allegiance to his country, his duty as a soldier; declaring that, if the stronger party prove recreant to the marriage vow, the weaker will no longer be bound by it; that if he come not at once, he need never come; that she will never see him again nor recognize him as her husband or the father of her children. [113]

Soldier's dream of home C&I/LOC

[Today the "strain on the home front" is, to a degree, offset by numerous support groups, governmental, veteran, and private, to aid families of soldiers as well as assisting men in the field. Electronic communication is beneficial in easing the separation from loved ones and also connecting with society by providing access to current information and "live" events. Multiple deployments, however, do not encourage quick recovery from such disconnections.]

The framework in which wars are fought mattered in affecting mental stress. In terms of the Civil War, the conflict was personal and close up. Battling against one's own countrymen presented a conflict of values by fighting on native soil cherished by both sides. The enemy, essentially, had the same culture, spoke the same language, and shared a common bond born from the creation of the United States.

Civil War soldiers also had many deep-rooted connections with their adversaries from pre-war experiences. This included members from the same family living on both sides of the conflict, relationships begun from prior military associations, and many friendships that had been created in the normal course of life. Conversely, in a global war, killing enemy soldiers that spoke a different language, from a different culture, suppressed the personal aspect from the equation.

Conflict of values produced from fighting fellow countrymen was particularly evident under certain battlefield conditions. When armies were within voice range of each other but not actually fighting, fraternization was common. There were opportunities for armies in winter quarters, or at the siege of Vicksburg, or just after the battle of Cold Harbor, for example, where both sides could mingle, fraternize, trade news, tobacco, coffee, and even visit friends or relatives.

Trading between the lines. EF/*CWAR*

Fraternization was also influenced by the common bond formed between all soldiers—a bond created from the common experiences suffered from the perils of combat, the deprivations, and the isolation from society. Fraternization, however, only aggravated the mental stressor. During truces, men had to temporarily separate themselves from that which caused them to kill their fellow countrymen and soon afterwards shoot at the same men who had just been treated as friends. [114]

There is one interesting incident at Gettysburg depicting the conflict of feelings shown by one Confederate soldier towards an enemy counterpart and a classic contradiction between compassion and hate: Sgt. Joshua A. Bosworth, 141st Pa., in retreating from the Peach Orchard against Barksdale's attack on July 2nd, had fallen back about 150 yards when he was wounded. Bosworth reached a stone wall to gain protection from the attacking Missippians.

Sergeant Bosworth described a strange encounter when approached by one of his attackers: "I asked one of them for a drink of water; he gave it to me, but while I was drinking he was loading his gun. He said he hated our men, then went off about eight rods (44 yds.) and shot at me, but I happened to lay down so he did not hit me. The bushes were so thick I kept out of their sight." [115]

Despite any conflict of values regarding fighting former fellow countrymen, fierce battles could sometimes cancel out any such feelings and disintegrate into a killing frenzy as witnessed by a Confederate officer at Sailor's Creek, April, 1865:

> ...The battle degenerated into a butchery and a confused mêlée of brutal personal conflicts. I saw numbers of men kill each other with bayonets and the butts of muskets, and even bite each others' throats and ears and noses, rolling the ground like wild beasts. I saw one of my officers and a Federal officer fighting with swords over the battalion colors, which we had brought back with us, each having his left hand upon the staff. I could not get to them, but my man was a very athletic, powerful seaman, and soon I saw the Federal officer fall.
>
> I had cautioned my men against wearing "Yankee overcoats," especially in battle, but had not been able to enforce the order perfectly—and almost at my side I saw a young fellow of one of my companies jam the muzzle of his musket against the back of the head of his most intimate friend, clad in a Yankee overcoat, and blow his brains out. [116]

Effects of Mental Stress

I would rather be a coward than brave because people hurt you when you are brave. Edward Morgan Forster

Casualties in the Civil War were almost exclusively catalogued in terms of physical damage. But, as we now realize, war injuries were both physical and mental. Little information exists, however, on the depth of Civil War psychiatric casualties. The lack of documentary evidence is, in itself, revealing. It indicates broad unawareness to recognizing such ailments as a result of exposure to high levels of stress.

In the mid-19th century, the science of military psychiatry was in its infancy.

The terms "battle shock," "battle fatigue," "acute stress disorder," and "post-traumatic stress disorder" were not yet coined. Mental casualties were often unrecognized, not treated, or led to shameful accusations of cowardice, malingering, or desertion.

Union Surgeon-General, William Hammond, however, described a mental condition he called "nostalgia." This was a descriptive term associated with sufferers displaying an aimless comportment or a blank look on their faces. In 1864, for instance, Captain J. McEntire, a provost marshal, described the actions of one of his prisoners, Private William Leeds:

> He has been strolling about in the woods, and has procured his food from soldiers... He has a severe cut on his nose and *his eyes are in mourning for the loss of his character.*
>
> Since enlisting the previous January, Leeds had been trying to escape the Army of the Potomac: "We have not been able to keep him a moment except in confinement," his colonel wrote. On Christmas Eve 1864 Leeds was committed, under escort, to the Government Insane Asylum - St Elizabeth's Hospital - in Washington, D.C.... [Italics added]: [117]

A modest number of nostalgia cases and a greater number of nostalgia-like patterns of behavior existed in Civil War armies. According to one study, "These cases were almost invariably generated during prolonged periods of inaction between episodes of significant combat. It was consistently observed that the symptoms tended to disappear whenever troops prepared for action and left their encampments to march toward the enemy." [118]

Another type of mental casualty recognized in the Civil War involved soldiers who simply gave up and ceased to be effective participants. Symptoms appear to have originated in the mind but resulted in physical conditions such as high heart rates and palpitations. Those afflicted were weakly and unable to perform prolonged physical tasks. Doctors observed many soldiers with cardiac conditions which were difficult to explain or diagnose. This condition became known as "soldier's heart," "effort syndrome," and finally as "DaCosta's syndrome." [119]

Mental injuries are, of course, produced from all wars. It is asserted, however, that, in general, Civil War soldiers saw greater destruction, experienced larger masses of casualties, viewed battles in greater proximity to the enemy, and surpassed the exposure to mental shock of others in later conflicts.

That few Civil War records exist regarding mental injuries may indicate more than the prospect that these ailments just weren't recognized. It might be that these mental afflictions were less prevalent than in later wars. Later conflicts were characterized by mechanization, more powerful weapons and ammunition, indirect fire, and frequent night fighting. Modernization in transportation and supply allowed battles to last far longer than those of the Civil War. Extended bombardments lasted for weeks, both day and night. Prolonged battles with fierce artillery fire tied soldiers to their positions preventing them from coping with situations in a direct manner. Their static condition, coupled with seeing casualties mounting all around, tested their mental stability and brought many to the breaking point. [120]

Mental Effects: Short Term

The mental effects of stress can be temporary or long-lasting. Combat stress, relative to the more severe versions, was short term. Its symptoms included fatigue, slower reaction times, indecision, disconnection from one's surroundings, and inability to prioritize. Most notably, the condition decreased fighting efficiency.

As mentioned earlier, many soldiers in Civil War battles were physically drained beforehand just to get to an action. Someone who is physically stressed is usually annoyed as well. The high state of awareness needed for combat added to the tension. It upset emotional balance and drifted towards behavior prone to irritation or anger, even over minor matters. Sleep deprivation magnified the imbalance even further and altered the mental capacity to make decisions that would otherwise be inappropriate.

Urgent situations, especially, can obstruct fear management, interfere with making sound decisions, and short-circuit rational behavior. Lt. Col. Charles H. Morgan, stationed at General Meade's Gettysburg headquarters when the July 3rd cannonade began, attested to an example of short-circuited decision-making when he wrote:

> Army headquarters were visited with such a shower of projectiles that sixteen horses belonging to the staff and escort were killed before the officers could get away and 'they stood not upon the order of their going.'
> One of them, seeing his horse badly wounded by a piece of shell, rushed into the house for his pistol to put the poor brute out of pain and coming out, put two bullets into a fine uninjured horse belonging to Capt. [James S.] Hall, signal officer of the 2d corps, and would probably have emptied his revolver as he was a poor shot, had not Capt. Hall interfered. [121]

In the Richmond campaign in 1865, Union Maj. Gen. Gouverneur K. Warren, commanding 5th Army Corps, reported:

> In the meantime several hundred men from the Second Brigade, First Division, had fallen back in great disorder, their officers having no control of them whatever. With the assistance of several officers, this mass of men was halted and faced to the front.
> Some straggling shots coming over, these men became frightened and

commenced firing into our own troops who were in their immediate front. Very many of the men fired almost perpendicularly into the air. They then broke and ran panic-stricken to the rear. One brigade of General Wheaton's division of the Sixth Corps was on the ground at this time, but their presence availed nothing toward stopping the flight of the fugitives. [122]

Mental Effects: Long Term

The long-lasting version of combat stress is known as acute stress disorder, post-traumatic stress disorder, or PTSD. For many, this condition would last a lifetime. Symptoms include depression, excessive irritability, guilt (for having survived while others died), recurrent nightmares, flashbacks, and overreactions to sudden noises. [123]

Undoubtedly, many have been damaged by their ordeal in war. However, according to one modern-day veteran, recent studies on PTSD by behavioral scientists have concluded that:

> ...the trauma of war strengthens rather than weakens us. They call it post-traumatic growth.
> We know that a near-death experience makes us better leaders by increasing our self reliance, resilience, self-image, confidence and ability to deal with adversity. Combat veterans tend to approach the future wiser, more spiritual and content with an amplified appreciation for life. [124]

Gerald Linderman's *Embattled Courage*, observed that the consequence of Civil War soldiers was difficult to analyze because of their silence. He notes that:

> In the war, wounds had been suffered by some and not by others; the problems they created were thus the concerns of the individuals involved, not of society. The soldier had wished to rid himself of the effects of body wounds as rapidly as possible; the veteran would do everything he could to accelerate the disappearance of mind wounds. Disturbing memories were to be kept to oneself, not to be aired publicly to relieve the sufferer and certainly not to correct public misapprehension of the nature of combat. [125]

The essence of this view answers the timeless question regarding the silence from all combat veterans of all wars: How could they ever begin to convey to those civilians with their own inaccurate vision of war, the indelible and painful physical and mental stresses they endured?

The reticence to discuss their ordeal was mistakenly viewed by the unenlightened at home as "heroic modesty." [126]

Coping:
Learning and Adjusting

So how *did* soldiers cope with fear? Was everyone afraid? Was anyone unafraid? Combat veterans will often state that anyone who has been in battle and said they were not scared is a liar. Men in combat, however, were not always afraid and not all were afraid at the same time. After speaking to a large group of college students about the soldiers of World War II, historian Stephen Ambrose commented about his audience's reaction: "[The students] were dumbstruck by descriptions of what it was like to be on the front lines. They were even more amazed by the responsibilities carried by junior officers and NCOs who were as young as they. Like all of us who have never been in combat, they wondered if they could have done it—and even more, they wondered how anyone could have done it." [127]

All soldiers knew they would experience fear in combat. Most learned to manage it. Most, naturally, tried to conceal it. Hiding one's fear was especially difficult for officers who must exemplify courage under fire. Leaders had the dual chore of controlling their own emotions and deal with those of their subordinates.   A Confederate artillery major described his experience at Gettysburg in the attack against the Union right July 2:

> One of the horrors of the thing, during a large part of the ride, was that I could see almost every shell that passed, as they were coming straight toward me, and their propulsive force was pretty well exhausted. As I approached the points at which the fire was directed, while I could not see so large a proportion of the shells, and this strain was of course diminished, yet the number of projectiles and explosions increased— until at last there was absolutely no separation between the reports, but

the air was rent by one continuous shriek of shell and roar of explosion, and torn with countless myriads of hurtling fragments.

When a man is undergoing an experience like this he does not think—his entire conscious being is concentrated upon the one point of endurance. But unconsciously, inadvertently, he may receive powerful impressions and bear away with him vivid and unfading mental photographs. [128]

Unless soldiers found ways to counteract fear, the result was disabling. There was no formula to apply in order to guarantee results. Every soldier had to discover his own way of coping—the process of managing taxing circumstances, expending an effort to solve personal and interpersonal problems, and seeking to master, minimize, reduce, or tolerate stress or conflict. [129]

Each soldier struggled inwardly to react to the combat experience as he saw it. A German captain from World War I, Adolph von Schell, once commented on his combat encounters: "Soldiers can be brave one day and afraid the next. Soldiers are not machines but human beings who must be led in war. Each one of them reacts differently, therefore each must be handled differently. . . . To sense this and arrive at a correct psychological solution is part of the art of leadership." [130]

In Paul Fussell's *WARTIME -Understanding and Behavior in the Second World War* he aptly states: "Physical courage is little more than the ability to control the physical fear which all normal men have, and cowardice does not consist in being afraid but in giving away to fear. What, then, keeps the soldier from giving away to fear? The answer is simply—his desire to retain the good opinion of his friends and associates...his pride smothers his fear." [131]

There were many ways which primed soldiers to manage their fears in combat. Some were natural reactions such as avoidance behavior. An example would be a soldier remaining on the battle line but minimizing risks by staying low, not fighting back, nor helping his fellow soldiers deal with the situation. On a more extreme level, individual soldiers might simply abandon their duties and run to a place of safety—an action justifiably deemed by those that remained on the battle line as cowardly. Leaving comrades deprived them of manpower to resist and only increased the danger to them.

But where is the dividing line between avoidance behavior and cowardice? The soldier that remained on the line and avoided danger was at least, present, but he was no more helpful than the one that left.

Motivation

Courage is not the absence of fear, but rather the judgment that something else is more important than fear. Ambrose Redmoon

There were a number of ways which aided soldiers in managing fear. Self-acquired determination helped. The most important tool in preparing men for combat, however, was training. It instilled the mainstays of coping with fear in combat: motivation, morale, and discipline.

Motivation is a force that provides the reason and willingness to perform and sacrifice. Morale provides the confidence to do it. Discipline provides the framework of behavior to operate. Besides the coping mainstays, there were diversions that drew soldiers' thoughts away from their emotions or men simply acclimated to their predicament and accepted their destiny.

Motivation sprung from several sources: within oneself, by being part of a group, by others' examples, or by prodding. It was the most important twin brother of tactical prowess. According to Morris Janowitz, in his work, *Professional Soldier*, this force is "based on a psychological motive, which drives a man to seek success in combat, regardless of his personal safety." This quest for success often leads soldiers to sacrifice with mortal results.

When this happens, the price paid, then, is the greatest irony of mankind—the willingness to engage in combat and surrender one's life for a cause that would never be enjoyed by the donor. Brigadier General S. L. A. Marshall, in *Men Against Fire*, said that, "if it were not for the ego, we could not make men face the risks of battle...Fears of varying sorts afflict the soldier in battle. When the infantryman's mind is gripped by fear, his body is captured by inertia, which is fear's Siamese twin." [132]

Motivation's characteristics are elusive. The willingness of soldiers to die for noble reasons, even the best ones, is not an absolute condition nor did it have permanence. In other words, most men were willing to take chances where death was not a certainty while their willingness to face danger did not remain a constant commitment. The level of fighting spirit required constant monitoring. Its highs and lows could fluctuate like a gust of wind if the troops' physical condition was depleted or their minds were not adamantly pledged to their work.

Commanders knew the supply of fighting spirit was finite. And even though this spirit was a restorable resource, the opportunity to apply it during an operation when it was at an acceptable level was rarely a controllable choice. Consequently, it was a key ingredient in a commander's judgment whether to engage the enemy or avoid it.

When engaged, the estimated value of fighting spirit even figured into which battle tactics to apply in specific situations. The value of motivation was not to be squandered on insignificant actions or sideshows irrelevant to a commander's main goals. Col. E. P. Alexander, Confederate artillerist, pointed out his concern over preserving soldiers' positive motivation in bringing on the battle of Gettysburg before the Confederate army was concentrated:

> I think it should surely have been a similar caution to that given
> General Ewell, on the afternoon of the first day's battle, when he was

directed to occupy Cemetery Hill but cautioned *"not to bring on a general engagement."* The principle involved in such cautions, which are often given, is not to waste the fighting spirit & power of the army on side issues. It is simply that of saving & concentrating every energy for the vital point at the critical time. This fighting spirit in the troops, after a period of rest, is something as real, though not as tangible as ammunition, & should be economised in the same way.

Even the best divisions, after one really severe & bloody action, cannot be expected to exhibit the highest development of spirit, particularly on the offensive, until after a little rest; during which new officers & fresh leaders among them acquire influence, & replace those who have been lost. Note the better spirit of Pickett's fresh division in his charge than that of the troops badly cut up two days before. [133]

On the Union side as well, General Meade, in his testimony afterwards, expressed his concern over the level of his army's fighting spirit after two days of heavy fighting at Gettysburg. He was anxious to appraise his troops' fighting spirit in order to judge what his next move should be. Meade said: "My ignorance of the condition of the corps, and the moral condition of the troops, caused me to send for my corps commanders to obtain from them the exact condition of affairs in their separate commands, and to consult and advise with them as to what, if anything, should be done on the morrow." [134]

Self-motivation

Self-motivation started at home. There were many sources that sparked individual spirit, most of them abstract. Rendered into a general sense, they included a patriotic fervor to save the nation, fighting for a cause, preserving a culture, and protecting family and home. Such reasons were viewed as most honorable, as noble truths, and prime motivators, not just for those that joined to serve, but for the families and communities that sent their men off to war.

Some men, less motivated by such righteous reasons, simply joined because their brother, neighbor, or best friend did. Others joined to escape boredom and experience the adventure of this sweeping event.

Still other incentives revolved around less gallant motivations. Practical-minded men saw the situation more as an opportunity for their personal benefit rather than as performing a duty to their country: they could join up and take advantage of the wide selection of lucrative financial rewards in the form of bounties paid for volunteering; they could earn an attractive sum of money by substituting for others less willing to enroll; it looked good on their resume. If volunteerism or other incentives were never motives to induce those able-bodied civilians to spring forth and join the army, they still had the chance of being coerced into serving by being drafted.

Self-motivation to pursue victory was also fueled by a feeling of self-righteousness. During spring operations of 1863, in North Carolina, Union Brig. Gen. Henry Prince seemed to have discovered the source of his division's motivation: "...I think our soldiers, with a superior *morale* arising from the holiness of their cause, are superior in battle to the rebel rank and file, more steady and persevering, more coolly determined on retaining a reserve of energy and a few un-wasted cartridges for final exhibition, and to sweep the field." Both sides held this pious feeling and each thought God was on their side. [135]

The reasons to fight, as viewed by those back home, remained so throughout the conflict. They were, for the most part, detached from the remote battlegrounds their sons fought over. They did not experience the affects of combat and how they altered the motivations originally held by those now fighting. Those at home could never understand the world that their soldier-son now lived in, a life turned upside down.

Anxiety was another self-motivating force. It represented immediacy and a call to action. It overrode all the intangible, abstract reasons that inspired men originally. It was a catalyst to fight with resolve. In Sun Tzu's *The Art of War*, written about 300 B.C., he said:

> Throw your soldiers into positions whence there is no escape, and they will prefer death to flight. If they will face death, there is nothing they may not achieve. Officers and men alike will put forth their uttermost strength. Soldiers in desperate straits lose their sense of fear. If there is no place of refuge, they will stand firm. If they are in the heart of a hostile country, they will show a stubborn front. If there is no help for it, they will fight hard. Thus, without waiting to be marshaled, the soldiers will be constantly on the alert, and without waiting to be asked, they will do your will; without restrictions, they will be faithful; without giving orders, they can be trusted. [136]

Sun Tzu's advice contained important applications for the Gettysburg campaign. The Army of Northern Virginia, in the role of invader, was operating in enemy territory, isolated from a friendly environment, and vulnerable to the unknown. This, in itself, was sufficient reason to maintain a keen fighting spirit.

But, is this form of motivation more powerful than the motivation evoked in those defending home ground? Perhaps it is when adding to it the superior morale bolstered by the Confederate army's recent victories at Fredericksburg, Chancellorsville, and Winchester.

But the Army of the Potomac's level of commitment, despite any depressed fighting spirit from being bloodied in previous battles, was altered when it tramped onto home ground. Fighting to regain seceded ground in Virginia, or any other territory proclaimed as Confederate, did not generate the same passionate motivation as the kind evinced when home ground was at risk. In this case, it injected an immeasurable amount of defiance against an invading army and influenced Union troops to fight with unprecedented determination.

This same fighting spirit is evident in the South's ability to wage a war for four years, mostly on their own turf, against great disadvantages in manpower and material resources. The value of motivation born from victories must be weighed against the inspiration ignited in an army defending its homeland.

Group Motivation

Group motivation started with links from common backgrounds. Familiarity and common interests were instant bonds of solidarity which quickly advanced the goal of unit cohesion. Most soldiers fought alongside people like them in some manner. Many units were comprised of men with a majority from the same age group, the same ethnicity, from the same communities, or from similar occupational backgrounds. Many units included relatives: fathers, brothers, cousins, and in-laws. The 24th Michigan Infantry, for example, had slightly over 1,000 men; included were 135 sets of brothers.

While many believe that most soldiers were in their teens, the mean age was in the mid-twenties. *Fox's Regimental Losses* gives a profile of soldiers fighting for the North:

> ...The mean age of all the soldiers was 25 years. When classed by ages, however, the largest class is that of 18 years, from which the classes decrease regularly to that of 45 years, beyond which age no enlistment was received. Of 1,012,273 recorded ages taken from the rolls, there were 133,475 at 18 years; 90,215 at 19 years, and so on. The number at 25 years of age was 46,626; and, at 44 years, 16,070...
>
> From statements as to occupation, it appears that 48 per cent. were farmers; 24 per cent. were mechanics; 16 per cent. were laborers; 5 per cent. were in commercial pursuits; 3 per cent. were professional men; 4 per cent. were of miscellaneous vocations. [137]

The disparity in numbers that served in either army is difficult to reconcile. *The Southern Historical Society Papers* gives the following statistics:

- Three-fourths of northern soldiers were born in the United States.
- The ethnic breakdown lists the following:

Of the 2,778,304 total enlistments in the Northern army there were:

Germans	176,800
Irish	144,200
British Americans	53,500
English	45,500
Other nationalities	74,900

Negroes	<u>186,017</u>
Total	680,917

- Total of Southern soldiers   600,000
- There were 316,424 Southern men in the Northern army. [138]

Motivational Bonds from Group Experience

Ultimately, it was the military experience which forged soldiers' motivations into more defined reasons. Historian Stephan Ambrose, in discussing World War II soldiers, commented, "In general, in assessing the motivation of the GIs, there is agreement that patriotism or any other form of idealism had little if anything to do with it. The GIs fought because they had to. What held them together was not country and flag, but unit cohesion." [139]

Gustave Le Bon, 19th century French psychologist, observed that organizations operate on group behavior. Group action creates a collective mind and causes individuals to act differently. Group action produces a sense of power springing from its numbers. Le Bon stated that "its members lose sense of responsibility, feeling can be communicated within the group by an almost hypnotic contagion…The individual's conscious personality disappears, and an unconscious personality emerges: 'He is no longer himself, but has become an automaton who has ceased to be guided by his own will.'" [140]

Soldiers about to enter combat also had an immediate and local rationale that inspired them—self preservation through group cooperation. The best means of increasing the chances of survival was fighting alongside comrades as a unified force, to fight zealously, and overpower the enemy to win. Group membership provided the greatest source of motivation to sustain oneself.

Military life, universally, lends itself to group kinship. The dilemma soldiers faced created a natural gravity towards fellowship and the rejection of social independence. The restricted freedom of movement in the military, especially in Civil War armies, forced men to cooperate with one another when moving about in concentrated formations and, when not campaigning, dealing with the proximity of soldiers in everyday living.

To the benefit of commanders, group life suppressed independent thinking and fostered reliance on others. In doing so, it changed behavior patterns to where soldiers achieved goals that were possible only as a group. This transformation minimized the independent effects of those individuals that were physically isolated from others or detached in spirit and whose unconstrained thinking interfered with the ability to muster the teamwork necessary to complete a task. Fighting as a disjointed team was at odds with the aim of self-preservation. It only increased the chances of getting wounded, dying in combat, or ending up in some prison camp.

As motivation evolved from the individualistic to a group approach, an inexpressible, everlasting bond developed from the shared hellish experience of war. The will to keep going was stoked by an unspoken covenant among men who shared the common life-threatening experiences of military life. Living through it was only made tolerable by the companionship and encouragement received from fellow soldiers. It was a bond above and beyond relationships already forged in civilian life.

One modern-day combat veteran succinctly commented on the power of group motivation which drove men to fight:

> …Those of you who have seen the face of war, understand: it's not really about loyalty. It's not about a belief in some abstract notion concerning war aims or national strategy. It's not even about winning or losing…
>
> Some of us have trusted our leaders, or maybe not. We might have been well informed and passionate about the protests at home, or maybe not. We might have groused about the rich and privileged who found a way to avoid service, but we probably didn't. We might have volunteered for war to stop the spread of global communism, or maybe we just had a failing semester and got swept up in the draft.
>
> In war, young soldiers think about their buddies. They talk about families, wives and girlfriends and relate to each other through very personal confessions… Patriotism and a paycheck may get a soldier into the military, but fear of letting his buddies down gets a soldier to do something that might just as well get him killed…
>
> Soldiers suffer, fight and occasionally die for each other. It's as simple as that. [141]

Rocky Bleier, former NFL star and twice-wounded Vietnam combat veteran, spoke of the unbreakable bond that grew out of the group experience: "We wear a common badge of valor and, like my fellow teammates, we will be forever linked together." [142]

Soldiers' devotion to military family was so strong it often created a sense of guilt for those leaving their unit when terms of enlistment expired. Even though they did their duty and performed honorably, many rejected the opportunity to muster out and made a praiseworthy commitment to remain in service.

Army structure also contributed to group motivation. Most Civil War soldiers were confined to operating within their basic unit, the regiment. On paper, it numbered about one-thousand men made up of ten companies of one-hundred men. In reality, attrition eventually averaged regimental strength to about 400. Soldiers' immediate interests were confined within the regiment, even though they fought tactically in a larger force of four or five regiments, the brigade.

The social importance to a soldier, his world of concern, however, started at the company level, and decreased upwards. The close-up environment of a company was the most basic social level where soldiers interacted and shared their common concerns and interests. They fought alongside one another; they

On parade. WT/*B & L*

suffered and died together, many of them buddies, hometown friends, or family members.

The buddy groups knitted this "band of brothers" into a steadfast team of men, crucial to operating and standing firm on the battlefield. The process created a competitive pride for soldiers within the company, the regiment, the brigade, and the division. Pride of association extended even at the highest level, the corps, where, in the Union armies, soldiers' uniforms proudly sported their distinguished corps badges.

Civil War tactics also provided a visual source of group motivation. Despite the fact that soldiers made attractive targets aligned in dense formations, being part of a fighting force arrayed in a line of battle was, in itself, an inspiring sight.

In November, 1863, in the Chattanooga-Ringgold campaign, Union Brig. Gen. Thomas J. Wood, commanding Third Division, described the beneficial effects of seeing the spectacle of one's own battle line:

> At 1:30 p.m. the arrangements were all completed, the troops were in position, and the reserve ammunition and ambulance trains in rear of Fort Wood. Then, at the bugle signal, the magnificent array, in exact lines and serried columns, moved forward. It scarcely ever falls to the lot of man to witness so grand a military display. Every circumstance that could heighten the interest of, or impart dramatic effect to, the scene was present.
>
> On the ramparts of Fort Wood were gathered officers of high rank, covered with honors gathered on other fields. There were also officers distinguished for scientific attainments and rare administrative ability.
>
> Troops in line and column checkered the broad plain of Chattanooga, in front plainly to be seen was the enemy so soon to be encountered in deadly conflict. My division seemed to drink in the inspiration of the scene, and when the "advance" was sounded moved forward in the perfect order of a holiday parade. [143]

Attack on Cemetery Hill, Gettysburg ABG/*LICW*

Conversely, the sight of one's line disintegrating and fleeing to the rear could extinguish any will to remain and have a stampeding effect on the entire force. The Union retreat through Gettysburg on July 1st provides an example. Large bodies of the Union troops were throwing down their arms and surrendering, in disorganized and confused masses. They were wholly powerless either to check the movement or return the fire. As far down the lines as the eye could see, the Union troops were in retreat.

Motivation by Others

Courage is contagious. When a brave man takes a stand, the spines of others are stiffened. Billy Graham

Another source of motivation was encouragement through respect for noble leaders. The respect shown Gen. Robert E. Lee, for example, is unsurpassed. Despite the Army of Northern Virginia's perpetual tattered condition and extreme deprivation, it is a challenge to name another army in history which exceeded the willingness to follow a leader into battle and readily offer themselves for sacrifice.

Troops were also motivated to fight with purpose by the sight of gallant actions by their leaders and fellow soldiers. Men, often in view of thousands, frequently sacrificed their lives to save a life, pull off cannon, or engage against overwhelming odds without a reasonable chance of success. Many such scenes, as well as witnessing the tragic deaths of familiar men, had an immediate reaction in energizing and rallying the troops to new levels of determination and boldness, often producing positive results.

At Winchester, Virginia, June, 1863, Confederate Maj. Robert Stiles described an inspirational, but deadly, encounter:

Lee UI/B & L

> At one of the last positions we took in the fight—it may have been the very last—there passed before me one of those scenes which give a flash-light revelation of the incomparable greatness of war and the sublime self-abnegation of the true soldier. The fire of the Federal guns was very deadly and demoralizing, and the captain of the battery next on our right, I think the Louisiana Guard Artillery, came up the hill between his battery and ours to steady his men.
>
> He was a fine horseman, finely mounted, and might well have served as a model for an equestrian statue as he rode out between the smoking muzzles, and, rising in his stirrups, cheered on his gunners. At that moment a shell tore away his bridle arm high up near the shoulder. Instantly he caught the reins with his right hand and swung his horse's head sharply to the left, thus concealing his wounded side from his men, saying as he did so, "Keep it up, boys; I'll be back in a moment!" As he started down the hill I saw him reel in the saddle, and even before he reached the limbers the noble fellow fell from his horse—dead. [144]

Actions involving flags evoke the greatest motivations and trigger the most heroic deeds of any object on the battlefield. The colors were treated as a powerful symbol that represented the spirit of the unit. The flag commanded as much respect as any religious icon. Capturing this well-guarded emblem gathered the greatest recognition. In fact, more medals of honor were issued for capturing enemy flags or saving one's own than for any other reason.

Battle flags, located at the center of a unit, were a natural focus to draw the enemy's firepower and consequently resulted in the highest death rates for anyone near them. In his after-action report, Capt. Edwin Libby, 4th Maine, wrote:

> I would also bring to your notice for gallant and meritorious conduct Sergt. Henry O. Ripley, the color-bearer of the regiment, whose daring and gallantry won for him the admiration of all—thirty-one bullet holes being put through the flag and the staff shot off from his hands. His color guard all being killed or wounded, he waved his flag defiantly in the face of the enemy. [145]

Follow the colors. *UI/LICW*

Col. H. A. Barnum, 149th N.Y., spoke of the enemy's attention to his unit's colors during the early morning Confederate attack against Culp's Hill:

> [The enemy's] charges were most impetuous and his fire terrific. Twice was our flag shot down, and a rebel first sergeant, in a brave attempt to capture it, fell within 2 feet of the prostrate banner, pierced by five balls. Its record of the bloody contest is eighty-one balls through its field and stripes and seven in its staff. Each time it fell, the color-sergeant, William C. Lilly, spliced the staff, and again placed it upon the works, and received a slight wound in doing so. [146]

Other Sources of Motivation

There were other sources which maintained the spirits of combat troops. Battle triumphs were great contributors. Lee's 1st day's success at Gettysburg, for example, was a sound victory. This achievement didn't merely boost Southern morale, it corroborated the Army of Northern Virginia's self-assessment of its fighting prowess it had long held.

A sense of accomplishing a difficult task as a group was also a great reservoir to draw from in motivating men. Union Brigadier-General James H. Carleton, after a torturous trek across desolate country, commended his men on their feat of endurance. He was impressed by the hardship's effect on the spirit of the men:

> ...They have reached their destination and accomplished the object assigned them, not only without loss of any kind, but improved in discipline, in morale, and in every other element of efficiency. That patient and cheerful endurance of hardships, the zeal and alacrity with which they have grappled with and overcome obstacles that would have been insurmountable to any but troops of the highest physical and moral energy, the complete abnegation of self, and subordination of every personal consideration to the grand object of our hopes and efforts, give the most absolute assurance of success in any field or against any enemy. [147]

Morale

As for courage and will - we cannot measure how much of each lies within us, we can only trust there will be sufficient to carry through trials which may lie ahead. Andre Norton

Morale is the keystone of behavior. It determines how individuals or groups perform tasks while subjected to physical and mental obstacles placed before them. Motivation and morale, although interdependent, are different. Motivation, for the purpose of this work, should be thought of as a set of principles or willingness to performing an action whereas morale is the degree of confidence to proceed with such action. Morale, then, is a spiritual level of enthusiasm, confidence, or loyalty with regard to the function or tasks at hand—a sense of common purpose with respect to a group. [148]

Victories, of course, raise morale. They secure confidence in an army's fighting ability as well as acquire beliefs in the commanders who lead men into battle. Conversely, defeats destroyed morale, bred disenchantment with leaders, created a dismal outlook on the prospect of achieving a military success and a pervasive fear that the future entailed more sacrifices and losses without producing any progress.

Good morale, even in the ordinary day-to-day tasks within an army, was essential in maintaining security and well-being. In battle, steadfast morale was critical in making troops respond to directives. It was at least as important to an army, mentally, as the numbers of guns and soldiers were to it physically. One expert in the art of war expressed his great respect for the value of this spiritual state by noting that in military affairs, "the moral is to the physical as three to one." [149]

The Confederate government's Secretary of State, R. M. T. Hunter, expressed his enthusiasm over the state of morale held in the South and its valuable influence in combating enemy advances:

> The foothold which the U.S. troops at first acquired within the Confederate States is being rapidly lost, and the United States Government has given manifest evidence of its fears that its seat of Government may be wrested from it. This exhibition of strength on the part of the Confederate States which was so unexpected by its enemies proves that its *morale* is greater even than its physical resources for the purposes of this struggle. [150]

Optimizing Morale

There were a variety of methods used to optimize morale. One was to insure the men were cared for. The perception of how soldiers were treated by superiors had a great influence on performance. In 1944, Gen. Dwight Eisenhower commented about the American soldier: "The capacity of soldiers for absorbing punishment and enduring privations is almost inexhaustible so long as they believe they are getting a square deal, that their commanders are looking out for them, and that their own accomplishments are understood and appreciated." [151]

Some methods in the Civil War were simple but effective. One technique was alternating unit positions during a march. As mentioned earlier, no one in the middle or rear of a column wanted to eat the dust of those in front nor suffer the punishing sporadic stops and starts of those ahead. "For my own brigade," one Union commander commented, "...this stretching [of the column] too much demoralizes, and I hold it to be as important to let the two regiments alternate in having the lead as to do any one thing that can be named to preserve the *morale* of a command. It is just, and justice must be preserved, or the regiment which is always in the rear loses spirit." [152]

Another way to maintain proper morale was through organizational design. Soldiers performed best when operating in an atmosphere that provided

The long march. *JB/LICW*

association with those that had the same expertise. Soldiers with specialized skills, such as artillerymen, engineers, or signalmen, were more comfortable grouped among men with the same talents, common interests, and commanded by officers knowledgeable in their specialty.

This concept made sense but it was often overridden by more important necessities where specialists traditionally operated in a dispersed fashion. Sharpshooters, for example, often fought attached to other units. This spread their skills throughout the battle line and gave these crack shooters access to targets that would not otherwise be available if concentrated only at certain points.

The artillery branch as well, unlike concentrated infantry or cavalry units, operated in diffusion. Artillerymen were normally scattered among large numbers of infantry troops. Although placing guns throughout an army was essential for protection, it prevented the guidance and the enforcement of specialized regulations which could only be applied by a centralized artillery command. Lack of supervision promoted a lack of discipline and decreased proficiency.

Both Northern and Southern armies argued that reorganizing units by combining men with the same specialty training or talented skills was necessary

The sharpshooter. WH/*CWAR*

to maintaining morale. Its importance was discussed by Confederate Secretary of War James Seddon with Gen. Lee who objected to forming a regiment of engineers. Secretary Seddon, nevertheless, argued the point over Lee's objection:

A very prominent [objection] seems to be that the companies are to be collected together in battalions or regimentally, and, therefore, will not be on hand for service when needed by the division commanders. Is this objection well founded? In order to give dignity to the service, as well as *esprit de corps* to officers and men, will it not be eminently proper, whenever the army is encamped for any length of time, and no immediate movement or attack anticipated, that the companies should be brought together regimentally? It seems to me it is only thus that the field officers can have sufficient control and influence; only thus, in great emergencies, that these troops can be made to act harmoniously together in large numbers, and that they can ever be of service as armed soldiers.

If they are to be kept simply and always in company organizations, subject exclusively to the orders of the major-general commanding the division, the probability is great that they will rapidly degenerate into mere drudges, scarcely better than camp-followers, to be employed in menial service, burying the dead, &c. As a natural consequence, the better class of officers…will soon resign, rather than be attached to a non-fighting corps of very mediocre reputation. [153]

Self-importance created from association to a specific group affects morale in a positive manner. Visibly displaying this association provides a sense of pride and claim to membership in the group. In today's military, for example, members of the Green Berets, Navy Seals, or airborne soldiers proudly display their accomplishments through badges, insignia, emblems, or special headwear as signature parts of their uniforms.

Civil War soldiers were no different. Soldiers visually demonstrated unit pride by displaying distinctive flags, wearing special uniforms, identifiable symbols and insignia, or distinguishing items such as bucktails or feathers in order to differentiate their unit from others.

Union troops wore corps badges—identifying each soldier not just to his corps, but the color of the insignia identified him to his division. With a recognizable trademark, men beamed with pride in advertising themselves as members of units whose reputations were surrounded by legendary feats of bravery from past battles.

Not all units, however, were perceived to have a renowned fighting distinction. For these unfortunates, lacking pride in one's unit fostered a dispiriting effect on the morale of men attached to a group with a dubious standing among its peers. It forced its members to parade around, to their discomfort, sporting an emblem or uniform that others saw as an object for ridicule and shame.

In the opinion of one commander, Union Brigadier General George Gordon, temporarily commanding 1st Division, 11th Corps, the humiliation attached to a simple emblem, a corps badge, was so pervasive, a major reorganization of the entire unit was recommended to eliminate the problem. In his view, disbandment was more practical than rehabilitation. Soon after Gettysburg, Gen. Gordon recommended dissolution of the 11th corps in the most no-nonsense manner which also, in effect, censured its corps commander, Major General Howard. Gordon's communication to Howard bluntly said:

> The reputation of this corps in this army is so bad that good troops are demoralized and rendered worthless while they wear its badge and form part of its organization. That its reputation is bad is patent to all. It is so from its disgraceful record at Chancellorsville, and not a clean reputation at Gettysburg; from its lack of discipline; from its un-soldierly education; from its great number of poor and worthless officers. The great number of skeleton regiments that form part of the corps is large enough to demoralize the conscripts that enter it, but not good enough to make them soldiers.
>
> The stigma of the corps attaches to all. New men enter it with reluctance, and remain in it from compulsion, with dejection and indifference; it is a fate which they must bear, but under which they break. These facts can be abundantly proved.
>
> I see no remedy for the salvation of the *matériel* of this corps, but the breaking up of the organization, its name and symbol cast into oblivion, the consolidation of its regiments into other corps, and pretty general dismissal of officers now or hereafter, as they shall, under other influences, prove themselves still worthless....
>
> In plainly expressing my views of this corps, I do not attribute blame to anyone in particular. I think it has had such unfortunate commanders that not even the ability of its present chief, nor any other, can remove the

opprobrium that attaches to being a member of the Eleventh Corps, Army of the Potomac. [154]

Conscious efforts by perceptive officers to affect morale were endless and creative. The presence of senior officers at the front was always reassuring. Visibly sharing the danger gained the respect of the men. In a more conventional example, General George Patton, of World War II fame, illustrated an attempt to manipulate soldiers' morale by providing interesting suggestions on ways officers could affect enlisted men. "In cold weather," Patton said, "General Officers must be careful not to appear to dress more warmly than the men." He also had advice for maintaining morale among his troops through conspicuous and frequent "inspirational" visits to the front:

> The more senior the officer who appears with a very small unit at the front, the better the effect on the troops. If some danger is involved in the visit, its value is enhanced.
> When speaking to a junior about the enemy confronting him, always understate their strength. You do this because the person in contact with the enemy invariably overestimates their strength to himself, so, if you understate it, you probably hit the approximate fact, and also enhance your junior's self-confidence. [155]

[Gen. Patton also suggested that high ranking officers should be flamboyant in going to visit the front but then avoid being seen going to the rear.]

Grant in the Wilderness. *UI/B & L*

Morale's Elusiveness

The state of an army's morale was elusive—temporary in nature, an unstable condition of the spirit. It was merely a snapshot in time gauging how men felt at that moment. It was not a quantitative measurement. It could not be measured with a meter or a stick, nor could it be inventoried like the summary of an army's firepower or troop strengths. This intangible commodity fluctuated more like a political poll, difficult to appraise at any specific moment. Even then, any estimation of its value was burdened with uncertainty.

Throughout the war, leaders fretted with the state of soldiers' morale and its effects on operations. Commanders made important decisions based on evaluating the commitment of their men; its assessment often determined the appropriate tactical moves. An army pumped with high morale could easily be persuaded to launch an offensive attack. The highest state of morale caused men to perform almost superhuman acts individually, in groups, or on a scale involving large numbers of soldiers such as Pickett's Charge. Major Thomas Osborn, Union artilleryman, shared his impression of Pickett's Charge. He reflected the respect he held for the men in gray and the powerful influence of morale that spurred men into an almost certain death:

> Taking it all in all, Pickett's charge, although a failure, was the grandest of them all. Although they were our enemies at the time, those men were Americans, of our own blood and our own kindred. It was the American spirit which carried them to the front and held them there to be slaughtered. Phenomenal bravery is admired by everyone, and that Pickett's men possessed. [156]

Equally, an army dejected and without dash took all the leadership skills available to keep it on the line and prevent an unordered retreat. Leaders did not move confidently without calculating the value of their force's self-confidence. Confederate Lieutenant-General Stephen Lee remarked how the state of morale immobilized his force in Georgia:

> As a corps commander I regarded the *morale* of the army greatly impaired after the fall of Atlanta, and, in fact, before its fall the troops were not by any means in good spirits. It was my observation and belief that the majority of the officers and men were so impressed with the idea of their inability to carry even temporary breast-works that, when orders were given for attack and there was a probability of encountering works, they regarded it as recklessness in the extreme.
>
> Being impressed with these convictions they did not generally move to the attack with that spirit which nearly always insures success. Whenever the enemy changed his position, temporary works could be improvised in less than two hours, and he could never be caught without them. In

making these observations, it is due to many gallant officers and commands to state that there were noticeable exceptions, but the feeling was so general that anything like a general attack was paralyzed by it. [157]

At Centreville in 1862, Union Major-General Hooker, division commander, adamantly opposed committing his men in their dejected state of mind:

It is my duty to report for the information of the major-general commanding the corps that my division is in no condition to meet the enemy. This was communicated to me yesterday by my brigade commanders, and on inquiry I find their *morale* to be such as to warrant me in entertaining the most serious apprehension of their conduct in their present state. I ascribe this great demoralization in the men to the severe losses they have sustained in battle, both here and on the Peninsula. They are in no condition to go into battle at this time. [158]

At Antietam, Union Maj. General Joe Hooker judged that his 1st corps did not have the correct morale level to attack Confederate forces: "Fully conscious of my weakness in number and *morale*, I did not feel strong enough to attack him in front, even after the arrival of the First Corps." [159]

Also at Antietam, General Meade gauged the steadfastness of his men when he chose what he thought to be the best tactical approach. He communicated his advice to Gen. McClellan: "To resist an attack in our present strong position I think they may be depended on, and I hope they will perform duty in case we make an attack, though I do not think their *morale* is as good for an offensive as a defensive movement." [160]

Union General Abner Doubleday noted the importance of the morale factor in affecting his orders at Gettysburg:

[After capturing men in the railroad cut, July 1st], upon taking retrospect of the field, it might seem, in view of the fact that we were finally forced to retreat, that this would have been a proper time to retire; but to fall back without orders from the commanding general might have inflicted lasting disgrace upon the corps, and as General Reynolds, who was high in the confidence of General Meade, had formed his lines to resist the entrance of the enemy into Gettysburg, I naturally supposed that it was the intention to defend the place....

....A retreat without hard fighting has a tendency to demoralize the troops who retire, and would, in the present instance, in my opinion, have dispirited the whole army and injured its *morale*, while it encouraged the enemy in the same proportion. There never was an occasion in which the result could have been more momentous upon our national destiny. [161]

[Had Lee disengaged from his victory on July 1st to avoid a general battle, it could have easily destroyed morale gained by a departure.]

Appraising morale of experienced soldiers was less difficult than for untested troops. Veterans' initiation to "seeing the elephant" had passed. They heard the sounds of battle, smelled its odors, and viewed the destruction of men, animals, and property. Having veteran soldiers, at least, removed one great concern for commanders leading men in the action: the experienced ones knew what to expect and the unpredictability of initiation had passed.

Green units, conversely, had no track record and no reputation to rely on. Steadfastness and performance of men in their battle inoculation remained to be seen. Some post-battle critics have concluded that certain inexperienced units should not have been committed to a particular action. Perhaps their judgments are valid.

But there are many examples of heroic actions by units in their first battle that counter such observations. At Gettysburg, for example, there were entire brigades and lesser units yet to be impressed by what battles were really like. They had not yet earned the title "combat veteran." They, nevertheless, performed admirably. Stannard's Vermont Brigade, in their first action, swept across an open field to catch Pickett's advance into a deadly enfilade fire; Bigelow's 9th Massachusetts Battery stubbornly and heroically defended the forward line of Gen. Sickles near the Peach Orchard without infantry support and then pulled the guns off the field by hand.

How then, can commanders reliably appraise morale levels to make important plans? As one observer stated:

> Nothing is more difficult than to indicate, in precise terms, that complex of qualities, passions, prejudices, and illusions that at any given time make up what is expressively called the *morale* of the army. Like the imponderable forces of physical philosophy, it is inappreciable by material weight and measure. Yet, if difficult of analysis, it does not fail to make itself felt as a palpable power… [162]

There were, however, specific indicators in appraising morale levels. They were manifested in areas that commanders might draw conclusions. The number of casualties—killed, wounded, and missing—might indicate willingness to fight.

Sometimes, statistics of losses in battle do not always indicate fighting spirit. The circumstances in which these casualties were sustained must be considered in the interpretation. Mistakes of officers or surprises caused by poor vigilance may have caused unnecessary losses. Blunders then fostered deliberate misstatements for the purpose of concealing misconduct.

While number of deaths provide an absolute figure, wounded and missing numbers are less certain in accuracy. Wounds were not always reported. The interpretation of reportable wounds was subjective and it was not unusual for such figures to be deliberately misstated. General Lee once remarked, "that [casualty reports] usually embrace all the slightly wounded, even such as remain on duty, under the impression, commonly entertained, that the loss sustained is a measure of the service performed and the danger incurred." A commander, for example, whose men participated in a minor way in an important battle but anxious to be associated with it, might embellish his unit's role by overstating casualty figures. Conversely, a commander that got "whipped" in an action may understate his losses to deflect the stigma of defeat that might otherwise reflect on his leadership and the performance of his men. [163]

Casualties classified as "missing" were even more unreliable. It was a generic term to cover those not reporting at roll call. They could be dead, wounded, or captured. A retreating force could not determine the fate if its men left on the field it no longer had access to. Other components of the "missing" category would include deserters. During the battle of Gettysburg, there were a large number of rowdy Union troops in Frederick, Maryland on a drinking binge. These deserters would be classified as "missing."

Another morale indicator could be a comparison of units exposed to the same battle conditions. Comparing a unit's high casualty figures in an action with lower ones of other units in the same affair could attest to the steadfastness of those units that suffered the most. Such figures, however, could also be deceptive. Archer's brigade in Pickett's Charge, for example, maintained the fight "after all reasonable hope of victory had vanished," yet suffered less casualties than other brigades. This result is subject to misinterpretation. Archer's men, with as much steadfastness as other units, advanced across a sector that may have escaped the effects of canister entirely while other units in the attack took the full brunt of the defenders. [164]

Fighting beyond the point of reason also elevated casualty figures. Doing this, however, merely reduced fighting strength without purpose. This was not an uncommon occurrence in war. Part of this could be attributed to an overload of high morale to the point where it became a liability. Feeling too pumped up with confidence needed to be tempered with caution since this feeling lent itself to a sense of arrogance or superiority by both soldiers and leaders.

A more reliable measure than casualty counts in determining the state of morale was revealed by the number of stragglers in the rear. Historian James McPherson noted that: "During the war a consensus existed that in many regiments about half of the men did most of the real fighting. The rest were known, in Civil War slang, as skulkers, sneaks, beats, stragglers, or coffee coolers. They 'played off' (shirked) or played sick when battle loomed. . . . Some deserted for good. Some really were sick much of the time." [165]

Stragglers were, most often, collectively described as cowards avoiding their duty. Excepting those that truly suffered physically from forced marches, they were rarely described with any degree of compassion. This generalization, however, does not consider that some were truly suffering from the mental effects of battle stress. Many evoked the same symptoms equivalent to World War II battle fatigue.

Sometimes, stressed Civil War stragglers were seen as sitting under trees, trembling, holding their weapons, jumping at loud noises or blankly staring into the distance. Devoid of any soldierly behavior, they were ineffective until gathered up, rehabilitated after a few weeks, sent back to their units, and presented as fit for combat. It is estimated that after the initial battles at Antietam or Sharpsburg, Maryland, one-third of the Southern force was absent due to straggling. [166]

The number of desertions was another morale indicator. Towards the end of the war southern morale had plummeted. Confederate General Preston reported "that there are over 100,000 deserters scattered over the Confederacy; that so common is the crime, it has in popular estimation lost the stigma which justly pertains to it..."

J. A. Campbell, Assistant Secretary of War, summarized the causes:

Straggler in the line of march.
ACR/*B & L*

> Exposed to the most protracted and violent campaign that is known in history, contending against overwhelming numbers, badly equipped, fed, paid, and cared for in camp and hospital, with families suffering at home, this army has exhibited the noblest qualities. It sees everywhere else disaster and defeat, and that their toils and sufferings have been unproductive. [167]

Other indicators of poor morale were signaled by a rise in incidents questioning military authority. Open disobedience to orders or the disregard of regulations called for military discipline to check discord in the ranks. Griping soldiers may have also indicated poor morale. But then, complaining was a soldier's right and a tradition ever since armies first formed. During World War II, a familiar measure of morale for George Patton and other experienced generals was the number of men that reported to sick call.

Morale, then, is a complex, abstract concept. It was not affected exclusively by the scorecards of victories and defeats, but by an infinite number of factors or combinations of them. It could not be taught and instilled in men with any permanence through training. It wavered from the results of living conditions, physical exertions, and deprivations. It could be controlled, but not to the degree that it remained at a constant, adequate level.

One obvious factor affecting morale was the depth of soldiers' experience.

Experienced men perceive events differently than inexperienced ones. Another factor relates to events or conditions as perceived at that moment. The protective comfort provided by defense works, for example, influenced morale. While defenses shielded men and saved lives, they had a disabling affect on the fighting efficiency of soldiers. Confederate Major Robert Stiles explained:

> In my account of the campaign of '64, especially of Spottsylvania and Cold Harbor, in noting our first real experience of fighting "in the trenches" and behind "works," I failed to mention its tendency to demoralize the men.
>
> The protection of a little pile of earth being in front of a man and between him and his enemy, his natural tendency is to stay behind it, not only as to part, but as to the whole of his person. I have more than once seen men behind such a line fire their muskets without so much as raising their heads above the curtain of earth in front of them; fire, indeed, at such an inclination of their gun-barrels upward as to prevent the possibility of hitting an enemy, unless that enemy were suspended in the sky or concealed in the tree tops.
>
> So greatly did this desire to fight behind protection increase that I have seen men begin digging every time the column halted, until their commanding officers declared that any man caught intrenching himself without orders should be punished severely. It is fair to say that, after a while the better men of the army, at least, learned to use without abusing the vantage ground of earth-works. [168]

Good morale could vanish in an instant. It could quickly deflate the fighting spirit of soldiers from the inevitable consequences of combat—seeing deaths of fellow soldiers, beloved "invincible" leaders, or those with closely connected relationships. This depressed feeling could occur from a local action or even from losses at battles elsewhere.

The loss of close friends and relatives happened often and the cumulative effect only aggravated any attempts to restore proper morale. Occasionally, the pain of losing a loved one triggered further loss. Confederate Major Stiles described one such tragedy:

> There were a number of Yale men in the Twenty-first Mississippi, among others two brothers, Jud. and Carey Smith. We used to call Jud. "Indian Smith" at Yale. I think it was at Savage Station, when the Seventeenth and Twenty-first Mississippi were put into the woods at nightfall and directed to lie down, that Carey Smith, the younger brother, putting his hand in his bosom, found it covered with blood, when he withdrew it, and saying: "What does this mean?" instantly died. He had been mortally wounded without knowing when.
>
> Judson Smith went almost deranged; yes, I think altogether deranged. He bore his dead brother out of the woods. His company and regimental

officers proposed to send the body to Richmond in an ambulance and urged Judson to go with it. He refused both propositions. He kept the body folded to his bosom, and all through the night his comrades heard Judson kissing Carey and talking to him and petting him, and then sobbing as if his heart would break.

Next morning he consented to have his brother's body sent to Richmond, but refused to go himself. When the regiment moved he kissed Carey again and again, and then left him, following the column all day alone, allowing no one to comfort him or even to speak to him. So that night he lay down alone, not accepting the proffered sympathy and ministrations of his friends, and resumed his solitary march in the morning.

That was Malvern Hill day, and when the regiment, on its first charge, stopped ascending that fearful slope of death and turned back, Jud. Smith did not stop. He went right on, never returned and was never seen or heard of again ["suicide by enemy"].

The family was one of wealth and position in Mississippi, the father, an old man, and having only these two boys. When he heard of the loss of both almost in one day he left home, joined Price's army as a private soldier, and at Iuka did just as his eldest son had done at Malvern Hill, which was the last ever seen or heard of him, and the family became extinct. [169]

For veterans that did survive actions, even they suffered. Outliving others, many long gone, provoked continual feelings of depression, guilt, or the compulsion to seek revenge. [170]

Morale could also drop suddenly in more indirect ways. There could be an unexpected loss of rations, or dismal news from the many rumors that floated around an army. There could be unconfirmed reports that the enemy was outflanking the line or threatening the rear. It could also change simply by a subtle shift from a familiar fighting position to an unfamiliar one or the execution of a basic maneuver such as a change of front. Brig. Gen. Alexander Webb, brigade commander at the Rapidan/James River campaign, 1864 reported:

> ...I tried hard to push my line over the little depression in the ground I found to be held by the enemy. But my men had lost their dash. They had no feeling of confidence and had had time to discover that the enemy's line was overlapping my right. The change of front had taken from them all confidence in the line now assumed. No regiment in the line had on its flanks regiments of its own corps. [171]

Morale could drop from an unexpected action, a reversal of a successful task, or commotion in the line. During the Virginia campaign, 1864, Brig. Gen. William N. Pendleton, C. S. Army, Chief of Artillery reported: "The artillery being on the march in column toward Hupp's Hill, a small body of the enemy's cavalry charged the train on the right flank, and by their bugle blasts, cheers, horses' feet clattering, and pistol shots in the darkness, occasioned an incurable panic in the infantry, already seriously disorganized." [172]

At Corinth, Mississipi, 1862, Col. John Oliver, brigade commander, in his operational report said: "To the Second Brigade of your division is the honor due of checking the advance of the rebel host for a whole day, and...forcing the enemy to that point which soon destroyed their *morale*, and changed a fine army, flushed with the anticipation of a speedy victory, into a flying, disorganized mob, wild with defeat and frantic with terror." [173]

Also at Corinth, Union Brig. Gen. Thomas A. Davies, commanding 2nd Division stated in his report:

> All the men upon the line remained at their work, firing steadily and doing well, when that portion of Sullivan's brigade on our right, and which protected the right flank, gave way, and the limbers and caissons of Dillon's battery came down the road leading directly in rear of the house upon the full jump, running toward the town parallel with Colonel Sweeny's brigade, presenting rather an alarming appearance.
>
> The heads of the horses of the limbers and caissons of my artillery were about on a line with the road, and they became frightened and unmanageable, floundered about, and those of one or two limbers and a caisson ran away and joined in the race, all of them running through my reserve (the Twelfth Illinois and Eighty-first Ohio), running down several of the men, injuring 12 in the Eighty-first Ohio and 9 in the Twelfth Illinois, and throwing the two regiments into confusion. This communicated a stampede in the ammunition wagons in the hollow in the rear of the line, and they too started on the run to the rear. They were quickly brought into order by the members of my staff and myself and continued moving slowly to the rear. [174]

At Malvern Hill a Confederate artillery officer noted:

> The effect of [the Union army's] repeated bloody repulses [of Confederate attacks] can hardly be conceived. One fearful feature was the sudden and awful revulsion of feeling among our soldiers, inspired by six days of constant victory and relentless pursuit of a retreating foe. The demoralization was great and the evidences of it palpable everywhere.
>
> The roads and forests were full of stragglers; commands were inextricably confused, some, for the time, having actually disappeared. Those who retained sufficient self-respect and sense of responsibility to think of the future were filled with the deepest apprehension. I know that this was the state of mind of some of our strongest and best officers; in fact, I do not know of any general officer in the army, save one, who did not entertain the gloomiest forebodings... [175]

Although restoring morale lost from a reversal could not be done in the same time it took to create, a single victory, or a string of them, could quickly inject a great sense of achievement. Just prior to Gettysburg, confidence from a long series of successes by the Army of Northern Virginia was never higher. Following sound wins at Fredericksburg in December, 1862 and Chancellorsville in May, 1863, the Confederate army again defeated Union forces at Winchester, Va. Confederate losses were minimal, numbering 269 men killed, wounded, or missing, while capturing 4,000 Union prisoners, many small arms, 200,000 rounds of small-arms ammunition, twenty-eight artillery pieces, and three-hundred wagons loaded with supplies of all kinds. [176]

These Confederate successes, undoubtedly, created a sense of superiority over the Union army's capacity to fight and infused a feeling of invincibility which would come back to haunt Lee in making his decisions and assisting in his defeat at Gettysburg. Overconfidence that originated from successes had the effect of devaluing the enemy's fighting skills, maybe too much. It created a corresponding contempt for the enemy, and could cause commanders to make reckless attacks or take chances not ordinarily feasible.

An enemy flushed with a superior level of morale from recent triumphs could be tempted to overcome enormous odds, forgetful that it was taking careless risks in the process. This misplaced sense of invincibility could cause the deaths of more soldiers than necessary on both sides and without any positive results.

A counter-tactic to such an overzealous opponent was to remind aggressive enemy troops of their mortality by subjecting them to a damaging artillery barrage lest they make any foolish moves that helped neither side. It was safer to avert the enemy's attempt against enormous odds, which sometimes proved successful. [177]

Battle successes, while elevating morale, could not be stored and applied for later use when needed most. For some Confederates, morale gained from recent pre-Gettysburg achievements was not enough to offset any negative feelings caused by Lee's upset in Pennsylvania. Southern morale after Gettysburg was indeed injured, but it was still intact. After all, the army only lost one in a row. Perhaps it was an aberration. There would certainly be future opportunities to prove that this was so. And even after three years of hard fighting, for many in the Army of Northern Virginia, confidence in victory was unshakable. They still believed winning was probable. Some even believed Gettysburg and Antietam were overall successes.

The Army of the Potomac's victory at Gettysburg, on the other hand, was proof that it *could* win a battle. In the process, it helped conquer soldiers' fear of the enemy and confront it on more equal terms with new-found confidence. It purged low morale levels caused from the army's perpetual command changes, its chain of defeats, and helped restore its fighting energy. [178]

Morale as a Weapon

While earlier Civil War engagements were fought to achieve combat successes, post-battle morale, good or bad, was merely a by-product of the result. As the war progressed, however, destroying the enemy's morale became a primary goal. On a strategic level, it became more important than physically overcoming the opponent.

Gen. Lee increasingly relied on the depressed morale in the north and its growing anti-war sentiment to influence an end to the conflict. Likewise, General Grant knew he had to break Southern fighting spirit to advance the northern cause. Victories, whether perceived or real, according to Grant, "produced a *morale* which could only be overcome by desperate and continuous hard fighting. The battles of the Wilderness, Spottsylvania, North Anna, and Cold Harbor, bloody and terrible as they were on our side, were even more damaging to the enemy, and so crippled him as to make him wary ever after of taking the offensive." [179]

On a tactical level, the quickest way to demoralize enemy troops was to inflict casualties on their officers. The presence of mid-to-low ranking officers was essential in maneuvering, controlling, and inspiring the actions of troops in combat. Taking out officers disrupted the chain of command. Viewing the death or injury of a leader at crucial times shocked the men, removed any feelings of invincibility, and could completely demoralize troops needing direction and encouragement.

Confederate Major Robert Stiles gives an example: [180]

> [Beulah Church 1864] The first definite recollection I have...is of the breaking of Col. Lawrence M. Keitt's big South Carolina regiment, which had just come to the army and been entered in Kershaw's old brigade and probably outnumbered all the balance of that command. General Kershaw had put this and another of his brigades into action not far from where we had burned the house to dislodge the skirmishers.
>
> Keitt's men gave ground, and in attempting to rally them their colonel fell mortally wounded. Thereupon the regiment went to pieces in abject rout and threatened to overwhelm the rest of the brigade. I have never seen any body of troops in such a condition of utter demoralization; they actually groveled upon the ground and attempted to burrow under each other in holes and depressions.
>
> Major Goggin, the stalwart adjutant-general of the division, was attempting to rally them, and I did what I could to help him. It was of no avail. We actually spurred our horses upon them, and seemed to hear their very bones crack, but it did no good; if compelled to wriggle out of one hole they wriggled into another. [181]

Targeting leaders was an often used practice of sharpshooters. Officers made identifiable targets because of their actions or gestures. An entourage or any mounted soldier was viewed as a potential prospect. Also, officers' positions in a battle line were predictable when the unit operated according to prescribed regulations.

Despite officers making tempting targets for anyone wishing to "bag" a trophy, chivalry occasionally entered the picture. One Confederate artillery officer noted:

> At the battle of Port Republic an officer commanding a regiment of Federal soldiers and riding a snow-white horse was very conspicuous for his gallantry. He frequently exposed himself to the fire of our men in the most reckless way. So splendid was this man's courage that General Ewell, one of the most chivalrous gentlemen I ever knew, at some risk to his own life, rode down the line and called to his men not to shoot the man on the white horse. After a while, however, the officer and the white horse went down.
> A day or two after, when General Jackson learned of the incident, he sent for General Ewell and told him not to do such a thing again; that this was no ordinary war, and the brave and gallant Federal officers were the very kind that must be killed. "Shoot the brave officers and the cowards will run away and take the men with them!" [182]

Officers were killed and wounded at a higher rate than enlisted men. The following is a consolidated statement of officers of the Army of the Potomac wounded during the period from May 1 to July 31, 1864.

Rank.	Total.
Brigadier-generals	9
Colonels	9
Lieutenant-colonels	8
Majors	96
Captains	601
Lieutenants	1,043
Medical officers	5
Chaplains	2
Total	1,903

Enlisted men wounded	36,508
Ratio of wounded officers to enlisted men.	1-19.2 [183]

Pickett's division casualties at Gettysburg on July 3rd, an exceptional example, numbered 31 of 32 field officers, a 97% loss rate.

Officers were more resistant to surrendering than enlisted men and, consequently, placed themselves in hopeless situations that resulted in their deaths. This also explains why there were proportionately fewer of them in the "missing" category. Wounded officers also tended to stay at the front longer than wounded enlisted men, chancing further wounding or death. Alonzo Cushing, for example, a twenty-two year old Union battery commander, took the full brunt of Pickett's division at Gettysburg on July 3rd. He was first wounded in the shoulder by a bullet, then another in his testicles. He continued with his gun crew, giving orders, vomiting and holding himself together, when a third bullet entered his mouth, killing him instantly. [184]

High-ranking officers were frequently fully engaged in the fray. Generals not only led their men in battle, they died with them. They were either leading the charge or on the defending line encouraging the men. Such fatal exposure usually resulted in death or injury. Over half, 55%, of all Confederate generals [235 of 425] were killed or wounded in battle. Such casualties happened primarily from leading attacks. [185]

The irony of it all is that when commanders did go forward and fell in full view of their men, the intended purpose to rally them could have produced two very different outcomes: it could have destroyed morale, as mentioned above, or it could have inspired or angered the men to seek revenge.

Leading the charge. CEHB/*LICW*

Gettysburg alone wiped out a large portion of experienced, scarce military talent from the rolls of its officers. The Army of the Potomac had 15 leaders in its high command killed or wounded. In killed, it lost: one corps commander, Major General Reynolds; five brigade commanders, Brigadier Generals Weed, Zook, and Farnsworth and Colonels Vincent and Weed. In wounded, the Union command had: two corps commanders-Major Generals Hancock and Sickles, three division commanders-Barlow, Barnes, and Gibbon, and four brigade commanders-Graham, Paul, Stannard, and Webb.

For the Army of Northern Virginia, Gen. Lee reported 16 officers in its top command killed, wounded, or captured:

> Major-Generals Hood, Pender, and Trimble severely, and Major-General Heth slightly wounded. General Pender has since died...Brigadier-Generals Barksdale and [R. B.] Garnett were killed, and Brigadier-General Semmes mortally wounded, while leading their troops

with the courage that always distinguished them. These brave officers and patriotic gentlemen fell in the faithful discharge of duty, leaving the army to mourn their loss and emulate their noble examples.

Brigadier-Generals Kemper, Armistead, Scales, G. T. Anderson, Hampton, J. M. Jones, and Jenkins were also wounded. Brigadier-General Archer was taken prisoner. General Pettigrew, though wounded at Gettysburg, continued in command until he was mortally wounded, near Falling Waters. [186]

There came a time when the choice of exposing high-ranking officers to dangerous situations for morale purposes prompted the inevitable question, "was the loss of a leader worth the tradeoff for the morale gained by the troops?" "At desperate hours", Douglas Southall Freeman noted, "when soldiers most needed intelligent direction, many of their officers took chances more desperate and, falling, made disaster complete." [187]

Officers, accordingly, suffered the uncomfortable dilemma of choosing to preserve themselves, their valuable experience, their leadership skills, and brainpower to fight another day by remaining in a safer zone at the rear. Or, they could ride into battle, gallantly displaying themselves to rally the men to victory and, most likely, become a casualty.

No officer wanted the stain of being labeled a coward. In the Civil War epilogue, the slate is empty for the list of officers that led their soldiers from the rear and lionized for saving their valuable skills.

Discipline

Discipline was one of the crucial intangibles that determined the performance of soldiers in battle. It complemented motivation and morale as one of the mainstays in managing fear. It was the quality that allowed soldiers to withstand the physical and mental stresses of sustained operations and the sting of combat. It was the key to overcoming individual reactions for the good of the group. Most importantly, it overrode concerns for self-preservation [fear]. Proper discipline assured generals that men would respond to orders. It allowed maneuvering of troops in a predictable manner.

The foundation for establishing and maintaining sufficient morale in troops was laid out through intense preparations beforehand—by conversion from independence to blind obedience, instilled from hard training and drilling, and by membership to an organization that created esprit de corps. Training, if done successfully, was expected to produce a specific character or pattern of controllable behavior and moral or mental improvement.

Creating discipline was a lengthy process. It involved systematic activities to implant group submission or, in some cases, prod men by using the fear of harsh punishment. Conversion to group unity was accomplished through the complete suppression of individuality held within each soldier. [188]

Instilling discipline cancelled out individual personal values in favor of military tasks that were otherwise abhorrent to the individual. Specifically, soldiers, as civilians, were raised with values respecting life and property. Criminal activities such as homicide, destroying property, or stealing were detestable in society. As warriors, however, men must be willing to kill others and destroy valuable resources. In fact, killing other humans, arson, and stealing [foraging] were required—normal activities of warfare. Adjustment to war, consequently, was a dramatic shift to the diametric opposite of the innate values which decried such behavior.

The evolution of recruits into combat-ready soldiers demanded the need to impress unquestioning obedience. One Confederate officer pointed out its supreme and serious importance:

> Undeniably, the first lesson of the soldier's life, logically and chronologically, is obedience. There is no department, no business, no station, in which instant, implicit, blindfold obedience is so vital to safety and success, or enforced by such terrible sanctions. In military matters hesitation is disobedience, disobedience is mutiny, mutiny is death.
>
> The principle of the soldier's obedience is the principle of *obedience*, a principle very little understood and very much condemned in this day and land. It is this: authority is to be obeyed, not because it commands what is right, but because it has the right to command. One under rightful authority is therefore absolved from responsibility as to the policy or propriety or consequences of the command; his sole dignity, as well as duty, is to obey with unquestioning alacrity. [189]

Blind obedience to a leader's instruction was the ideal picture of military discipline and enabled officers to control the bearing and fighting posture of the unit. To conduct operations, commanders relied on their ability to maneuver thousands of men, in robotic subjugation, with synchronized skill, at least as good as the enemy's, during the chaos of a battle.

Union Gen. John Gibbon spoke of discipline's importance as his men were about to receive the approaching force of Pickett's division at Gettysburg:

> Few unacquainted with the rigid requirements of discipline and of how an efficient military organization *must* necessarily be a machine which works at the will of one man, as completely as a locomotive obeys the will of the engineer not in all things, but in everything which the locomotive was *built* to obey, can appreciate the importance of drill and discipline in a crisis like the one now facing us. [190]

Consider the discipline shown by Federal soldiers in the Union center as Pickett's, Pettigrew's, and Trimble's divisions transited the open fields on a path

Union advance near Nashville. EJM/*B & L*

aimed directly at them. What a temptation for the Union infantrymen to squeeze down on their triggers and obliterate the death threat that was about to confront them. A premature volley by some, however, could have unleashed a chain reaction down the line, wasting thousands of bullets, costing precious time to reload, emboldening the enemy advance by causing littler damage, and destroying the shock effect reserved for well-aimed firepower.

As it turned out, the advanced Union skirmishers reacted first. As they withdrew towards their main line, a few anxious soldiers began popping off a few rounds. Thousands, however, remained steadfast, waiting for the right moment. For them, it must have seemed an eternity as they waited for the order to fire. It wasn't until the enemy approached the Emmitsburg road that the line finally blazed away. That was discipline.

Proper conduct in battle was directly linked to discipline. Disciplined troops exhibited better behavior than inexperienced ones, especially when deprived of the protective cover offered by fortifications. They could hold their fire longer and were more willing to obey orders. Green troops tended to operate with excess caution, less willingness to fight, and less likely to leave protective defense works for an attack.

In close combat, however, early in an action, disciplined performance such as precision maneuvering learned from drill training was not a usual occurrence. Although training was the basis for establishing certain behavior, combat disconnected soldiers from the binding influence gained from instruction. Discipline could be held in check, however, by expressions of confidence from a respected leader and continuous involvement by a unit's officers.

There is an axiom stating that training is never finished or completed. In this regard, maintaining discipline was not a self-sustaining process. It required constant monitoring. Inattentiveness to enforcement caused discipline to evaporate quickly. Lax attention to regulations led to permissiveness followed by pervasiveness. If left unabated, it infected the entire army. Early in the Gettysburg campaign, the Army of the Potomac's General Order No. 62 exposed the existing discipline problems and how to deal with them:

> The lax enforcement within this army of certain orders deemed absolutely necessary to keep it in a proper state of efficiency, and their consequent non-observance, has been brought to the notice of the general commanding. It is not by multiplying and reiterating orders that this evil is to be corrected, but by a knowledge on the part of all officers of existing orders, and a determination to carry out their requirements not only within their own commands, but, as far as may be, within the sphere of their influence. This is as sure a test of capacity and fitness for military position as good conduct on the field of battle…
>
> The intervals between active operations should be used by every officer and soldier anxious to improve and advance himself and the success of our common cause, as opportunities for instruction and improvement in drill and discipline. All officers are expected to maintain a high state of drill, discipline, and efficiency within their respective commands, and when corps commanders are not heartily and thoroughly supported by division, brigade, and regimental commanders, on proper recommendation, such officers will be relieved from duty with this army. [191]

Training

At the beginning of the Civil War neither side was ready. The Confederate army was non-existent. The Union army was small, around 16,000, and poorly equipped. No one predicted the intensity or duration of combat. Quick and absolute victories were not to be. Major battles were followed by paused recovery periods for the armies to rebuild and await the next engagement. This cycle happened repeatedly and without progression towards a conclusion. Little ground had changed hands while the Southern government remained intact.

During the first two years of conflict, fighting forces were, in effect, sacrificial armies. Men were falling by the thousands. Although it was an expensive investment period in manpower and physical resources, time allowed commanders to learn to fight in ways that would eventually bring the conflict to a decisive end.

Previous warfare had never called for tactics of such magnitude. The scale of Civil War battles dwarfed any prior encounters for U. S. forces. The Mexican War, for example, lasted a year and a half; the battle theater, although far from home, was comparatively small and allowed decisive and conclusive victories to end the conflict. That war's total casualties were less than those encountered in three days at Gettysburg. The Civil War, on the other hand, lasted four years, covered almost the entire nation, and involved a million men in uniform at the same time.

Only one person in the military, Gen. Winfield Scott, had the experience of maneuvering a force of more than five thousand soldiers. Military commanders who were veterans of combat in Mexico and Florida could only draw from prior battle encounters and textbooks, both of which would be of limited help for the Civil War experience. Most commanders, in fact, had not even participated in basic operations at the lowest level of the battalion or regiment. In addition, outdated textbooks did not take into account the inventions of new weapons, improvements in ammunition, and other devices used in warfare. [192]

Training inexperienced officers and men to fight and win battles was a monumental task. Fortunately, they were volunteers and eager to learn. Volunteer officers were instrumental in easing enlistees' transition from civilian to soldier. They were pulled from the same society as enlisted men. Because they knew their men's origins, they were better equipped to represent and interact between their subordinates and those at home, to encourage men in training, and lead them in battle.

Volunteers made up the bulk of both armies. Naturally, they were supportive of the cause, patriotic in their nation's call to arms, receptive to discipline, and possessed character of sacrifice. Like their Revolutionary War predecessors, these gallant individuals would provide the army with many high quality, intelligent, and skilled men from all segments of society. Many proved to be superior to the professionals.

General Ulysses S. Grant, referring to General William Sherman's army of volunteers, wrote: "[This force] had sixty thousand as good soldiers as ever trod the earth; better than any European soldiers, because they not only worked like a machine but the machine thought. European armies know very little what they are fighting for, and care less." [193]

Training included the development of essential human aspects in the course of instruction. Officers learned to understand soldiers' physical limits, their needs, and how to spur them into action. Schooling was crucial in instilling motivation, morale, and discipline as well as developing important elements of physical preparedness that would help them endure a rugged military life and the perils of combat. [194]

The training routine included learning numerous operational regulations and protocols, achieving respect for the military exercise, and establishing bonds among soldiers. Instructions were devoted to mastering tactics, techniques,

New Recruits. WT/*B & L*

familiarization with equipment and weapons, and understanding the human aspect of fighting within a group.

The first and toughest phase of turning civilians into soldiers was getting new recruits to shed their civilian approach to life. It started with severing individuality, independent thinking, and the civilian culture recruits had experienced since birth.

Fresh enlistees were accustomed to lifestyles and choices incompatible with army living. As civilians, they possessed freedom of movement, the liberty to make independent decisions, the choice to remove themselves from danger, to act and overcome deprivations, and exercise control over their destiny as individuals.

Army life frequently entailed subordinating one's own political, social, and religious views in order to save their nation. It meant a divorce from physical comforts—food, shelter, healthful living, and an acclimation to the hardships and deprivations of military living. Enlistees were thrust into unfamiliar surroundings with strangers barking military terms they had yet to understand.

One officer described the experience:

> When a man enters the military profession, whether as an officer or a private soldier, by that very act he is cut off from the pursuit of his personal aims and purposes and devoted to the service of his country. Thereafter he has no home, no farm, no workshop, no business. He knows no self-directed future, attempts nothing, and expects nothing for himself. Every man outside the army regards him, and he regards himself, as a man relieved, separated from the entanglements and opportunities of the business world, and consecrated to a service which may at any time demand the sacrifice even of his life. [195]

Transported into the world of military culture, men were subjected to a life of regulation. According to one officer:

> The soldier breathes, as it were, an atmosphere of accountability. His daily routine is made up of inspections and reports. What he is, what he has, what he does, his person, his possessions, his conduct, are constantly passing under a scrutiny so searching that nothing escapes, however; trivial, and all must conform to unvarying "Regulations." This is perhaps the most prominent and impressive feature of the life. [196]

While a cultural shock for most, for some, the transition from civilian life to the military was a liberating and profound experience. Confederate Major Robert Stiles noted:

> The social atmosphere of the soldier-life is Freedom from Social Shams. The unconventionality and candor of student life are proverbial, and yet, though I stepped from the hearty, ideal student life of Old Yale into the ranks of the Confederate soldiery, it was not long before I felt that I had never before realized how unstudied, unconventional, and absolutely sincere human life could be. It was almost startling, the degree to which I knew other men, my comrades, and felt that I was known by them.
>
> All the little shams, insincerities, and concealments of ordinary society disappeared; until, for the first time in our lives, we seemed to be stripped bare of the disguises under which we had therefore been accustomed to hide our real characters, not only from the world in general and from our most intimate associates and companions, but even from ourselves.
>
> It was this which imparted to the religious life of the army a power and thrill unattainable, even unapproachable, in ordinary life. So close did men get to each other that I experienced no difficulty and no embarrassment in conversing with every man in the company on the subject of personal religion, and in these conferences have often felt that I was playing upon a naked human soul, between whom and myself there was absolutely no barrier and no screen.
>
> It was an experience thrilling and tremendous indeed. In view of it, I have more than once remarked that if my Maker should reveal to me that I had but a short time to live, and should permit me to choose a position in which I could accomplish most for the regeneration of my fellow-men, I should unhesitatingly say, "Let me be an officer in an army, in a time of active service." [197]

Military successes depended on order and discipline based on the single-mindedness of group action and not the individual approach. The transformation from civilian to soldier suppressed individualism in favor of one in which problem-solving was a team effort. While individual proficiency was critical to battlefield successes, it did not insulate soldiers from the effects of fear. Collective training helped build resistance to succumbing to fear's consequences.

Individualism, however, could re-emerge. If soldiers lost the trusting dependence of their leader's judgment, they quickly filled this command vacuum by their own single-mindedness. When this occurred men performed in response to their own best interests to survive. As military discipline evaporated, so did the chances of succeeding as a functional unit. [198]

The foundation for establishing and maintaining sufficient morale in troops was laid out through intense preparations beforehand—by conversion from independence to blind obedience, instilled from hard training and drilling, and by membership to an organization that created esprit de corps.

Major Stiles once posed a question to himself, "What…is the training and what are the formative elements and forces of the Soldier-Life? I answer:"

The essential character of the Soldier-Life is "Service;"
Its every employment, its all-pervading law, is "Duty;"
Its first lesson—Obedience unquestioning;
Its last lesson—Command unquestioned;
Its daily discipline—Accountability unceasing;
Its final burden—Responsibility unmeasured;
Its every-day experience—Hardships, Perils, Crises unparalleled;
Its social atmosphere—Freedom from Social Shams;
Its compensation—Fixed Pay;
Its inspiration—Promotion from Above. [199]

[Today, the U. S. Army recognizes the following "Army values": Loyalty, duty, respect, selfless service, honor, integrity, and personal courage.]

The Drill

The centerpiece of training was the drill. This activity, more than any other teaching tool, created teamwork and military discipline. It embodied the qualities learned from all phases of instruction. Drill training provided more than teaching men what to do and where to go in formation. It was an important exercise in group skills and obedience. It established a reference point of behavior for soldiers to follow. Through group participation, it established a base from which morale could be built on. The sight and sounds of the synchronized rhythm of massed troops in motion was, in itself, an uplifting experience. Being part of it was a positive morale booster for men within the ranks. It established confidence through proof of performance. It gave troops

Battalion drill. WM/*CWAR*

pride of accomplishment by the group's successful completion of complex maneuvers, and, most importantly, established a sense of unit cohesion that would be needed on the battlefield. Being part of a well-trained force "certified" soldiers' preparedness for battle. [200]

To learn the complex movements involved in the drill and attain the precision needed, regiments devoted intense efforts to prepare themselves for events that would depend on their tactical proficiency. Training was incessant. In the quiet season regiments drilled each morning and afternoon. They drilled for weeks, then months, then years to achieve precision and maintain their edge.

Besides creating teamwork and discipline, training in the drill had many practical purposes. Specifically, it taught soldiers how to move and evolve into different formations. It consisted of a series of movements that affected a unit's speed, direction, alignment, and arrangement of the formation.

Drill practice established measurable proficiency, a predictable period of time in which a commander could expect when his troops would arrive on the field, deploy into action, or reach a point of contact with the enemy. It took "60 minutes to form a division into line of battle" and "30 minutes to form up in a field after moving through a wood." Calculations could estimate the time necessary for advancing forces to move across an open field, predict casualties sustained in the advance, and figure the number of troops needed to carry the enemy's works. [201]

Predictability added reliability in gaining the advantage. Whoever arrived at the scene of battle first, for example, could choose the best ground to occupy. Whoever could deploy the greatest number of troops in battle formation first, increased the odds of winning. Whoever was able to position troops sooner to outmaneuver the opponent, gained an edge.

Through the drill, men were trained in the school of the soldier, which introduced the basic movements as an individual, and then the school of the company, which taught men to maneuver as a unit.

During operations, units moved about either in a column formation or assembled in a battle line. In a column, they moved four abreast; in a battle line they advanced or stood shoulder-to-shoulder, two lines deep. The column and battle line formations were the tactical basis for commanders to function during Civil War operations.

The rapid-changing nature of combat called for both column and battle line configurations. Evolution from one form to the other happened often. Evolutions required rapid responses to handle moves to other locations, or assemble and prepare for an attack. They required a high degree of teamwork and thoughtful planning to choose the proper timing of when to deploy as a column or when to operate in a battle line.

Having the appropriate formation for the current circumstance could be instrumental in saving the moment or gaining the advantage. Union officer, Joshua Chamberlain, wrote: "Rapidly changing plans and movements in affecting the single purpose for which battle is delivered are what a soldier must expect; and the ability to form them wisely and promptly illustrates and tests military capacity…Orders had to pass through many hands; and in the difficulties of delivery owing to distance and the nature of the ground, the situation which called for them had often changed." [202]

A tactically-proficient brigade commander knew when to perform the correct evolution to match the situation. The ground to be traversed, for example, was an important consideration. Passing through woods required a different style of movement than crossing fields.

A battle line formation could fight but it could not move well across terrain blocked with impediments such as a creek with only one bridge. A column formation, however, could move rapidly across a bridge but it was extremely vulnerable to attack and couldn't defend itself.

Men were trained to change direction, alter their type of fire, perform a measured pace of advance or withdrawal, fight in a variety of positions, standing, kneeling, or prone, and many other motions needed in the course of operations.

Instruction in the drill produced psychological benefits through group participation. Prussian ruler Frederick the Great, in describing the importance of the proficiency of the drill, said: "Part of the stress of battle stems from its puzzling and capricious nature: battle drills help to minimize the randomness of battle, and give the soldier familiar points of contact in an uncertain environment, like lighthouses in a stormy sea." [203]

The mental benefits produced from drill practice were at least as important as physical training. Each and every soldier possessed his own level of motivation.

Each had his own view on self-preservation, coping with danger, sense of patriotism, or level of willingness to achieve a goal.

These values changed, however, as danger increased or when closing with the enemy. It is said that one of the most embarrassing predicaments for soldiers in an attacking line was the point when their mental state that first prompted their willingness to participate in the attack was equal to their desire for self-preservation. At that stage the dilemma was to choose to continue forward or opt out in some manner. That quandary would occur anywhere in an action from the stepping off point to the point of contact.

Group participation instilled confidence and helped convince the men that they could perform as soldiers. Natural courage was not enough in persuading men that they could fight. The group must be made ready to willingly follow their leader into the jaws of death and be capable of withstanding sustained and severe battle action. Establishing confidence helped convince newly-trained, untested men that they could win in an activity that they had yet to experience.

The drill's repetitive training was intended to be branded into soldiers' memories in order to respond without conscious thought. Drill movements, once indoctrinated into soldiers' subconscious beings, helped deflect the initial shock of men experiencing their first battle. Conditioned reactions maintained order and were essential in sustaining soldiers in a chaotic setting.

Leaders expected their men to behave in response to their orders and without soldiers questioning the motives of a directive or anticipating their orders before they were delivered. Opportunities to think too much on any given action allowed the men to muddle the process by independently rationalizing or deciding on matters that were supposed to be handled by their leader. Frederick the Great once pointed out that if his soldiers were allowed to think, not one of them would remain in the ranks. [204]

The mechanical movements orchestrated from the drill helped overcome the anxieties of combat. Elevated stress could wreck the battle tactics of the best commander. Much of it was produced from the confusion of unfamiliar battlefields covered with smoke or obscuring terrain and the unpredictability of rapidly changing combat situations.

A well-drilled unit was much better equipped to suppress the fear of the unknown. A WWII British officer said: "Drill as the means to an end is indispensable to every army. It cannot be replaced by individual training nor by sporting instinct. A man must have obedience drilled into him, so that his natural instincts can be curbed by the spiritual compulsion of his commander even in the most awful moments."

Although relentless practice exercises in the drill was the centerpiece of training, learning basic elements merely laid the groundwork for performance. Training was devoid of many elements that would alter the reaction of men between what they learned during training and what took place under real battle conditions. [205]

Acclimating Civil War trainees for combat rarely included any attempt to teach realism of battle. Instructions for preparedness lacked important advice on what trainees would expect to encounter. Helpful training aids such as target practice or mock battle maneuvers conducted with any attempt to attain realism were practically non-existent. Experience in the use of the musket was, more than likely, gained from performing non-firing practice movements as prescribed in the drill manual.

Once engaged in the real thing, however, commanders could hardly rely on the drill to carry their men entirely through a battle. It was expected that each man would face the initial exposure to action in his own way. Each was expected to do their duty, overcome their fear, and come to grips with the possibility of being killed or wounded.

Today's military training, in contrast, incorporates many elements not available to Civil War trainees. Major Gregory A. Daddis, U.S. Army, described some of them:

> Controlling fear is within reach of well-trained units. Realistic, demanding training provides a soldier advantages in the struggle of natural instincts for self-preservation against real or perceived threats...
>
> Incorporating battlefield stimuli—the sights, sounds, and smells of a firefight—into training makes training real. Combat affects soldiers violently, and they must be conditioned to deal with their fear. If training can condition a soldier to kill, then training can condition him to cope with fear. The key is not desensitization but sensitization. Soldiers need to know how their minds and bodies will react to fear and develop a combative mindset that mitigates the psychological and physiological effects of fear. [206]

Linear Tactics

Linear tactics provided a tangible benefit to Civil War soldiers in overcoming their fear in battle. Body contact, elbow to elbow or shoulder to shoulder, provided the connective control essential in preserving unison and integrity. It gave each soldier a point of reference for orchestrated movements. Without such a bond, the once smartly-dressed lines at the start would quickly evaporate into a ragged disjointed formation of men lacking the discipline needed to maneuver and fight effectively. The touch provided an extra "set of eyes" on each side. Men did not have to look to see if they were aligned properly with an adjacent soldier, they could feel it.

The linear formation is where soldiers would be tested the most to prove their mettle. It was two-lines deep with a third line of fewer troops immediately to the rear called file-closers. By regulation, the space between the front and rear fighting rank was thirteen inches.

This compact space was challenging. Soldiers were compelled to work under a

Cold Harbor. EF/*LICW*

restrictive state of movement. Elbow room to load muskets with drawn ramrods was limited. Troops were expected to aim and fire their weapons accurately while, at the same time, being jostled by a constant bumping and brushing against adjacent soldiers making the same motions.

Besides that, linear tactics also contained inherent problems in control. Maintaining the integrity of a standard two-line formation required a great deal of attention and discipline. There was a natural inclination for men to drift from a formation's good lines into bunches. Some men, more rambunctious than others, tended to move boldly forward while those less daring were satisfied to cluster behind them.

In addition, soldiers were of different heights and took different lengths of steps. Such variations soon separated them from any soldier moving at a different stride. A line too loosely connected caused a wavering effect which reduced the line's field of fire.

Loose formations, however, especially ones made up of veterans, could still allow a coordinated advance, but only slowly. According to Halleck's *Elements of Military Art and Science*, when a loose-order line moved too quickly, the formation broke, forming "great and dangerous undulations." This disorder caused further problems when successive lines intermingled and command structure was destroyed.

The faster the ordered pace of the attack, the more the problem accelerated.

One can imagine the results of a line moving at the fastest tactical pace, the double quick—165 steps per minute [almost three per second]. The view would be one of an incoherent mob and, if the pace lasted more than a few minutes, the fighting force was too drained to fight effectively. [207]

Green troops were less proficient in loose formations. They seemed more focused on keeping the line dressed and compact. The novices possessed what one historian called "that anxious effort to preserve the alignment." They had not yet learned the ways of battle nor had they welded the brotherhood bond created from combat to feel comfortable about losing physical contact with their comrades. [208]

In his book *Pickett's Charge*, George Stewart commented about the two-line formation:

> There has been nothing more awkward under the sun than one of these long double-ranked lines, nothing more difficult to move properly from place to place, with necessary changes of direction and adjustments to the movements of other equally awkward lines—especially under battle conditions.
>
> ....The second great tactical problem arose from the necessities of terrain and cover which had dictated that the troops be drawn up in two bodies. Heth's right was about a quarter-mile behind and to the left of Pickett's left. Unless the two could be united, there would be two separate and weak attacks, lacking the destructive impact of a single strong one.
>
> ...The importance of having a precise objective—in this case, the clump of trees—should here become apparent. Obviously, to say that it was the objective does not mean that every Confederate soldier was instructed to march right at it. Instead, it was the point toward which the right of Heth's division would advance, and toward which...the left of Pickett's division would direct itself. [209]

Although linear tactics used in the Civil War are often ridiculed as a wasteful commitment of fighting men, they gave the Civil War soldiers something that future soldiers, who employed loose-order formations, did not have—the comfort from feeling his fellow soldiers physically near him, of others sharing mutual danger, of seeing comrades fall and making sure someone had cared for them.

A soldier's physical proximity to his comrades had the great benefit of improving fighting morale, staying power, and proved to be an important coping mechanism. Closeness to others in battle was preferred. The "touch" gave strength and support to members of the regiment and repeatedly telegraphed to each soldier the fact that they were not alone. The group experience created the feeling of membership to a body linked to achieving the same objective, to acting as a united whole.

Personal closeness was driven by a potent psychological desire to dismiss the isolated and empty feeling experienced by combat soldiers. The comforting thought was the simple fact that they, as soldiers, were not alone to navigate through their terrorizing experience. Soldiers in formation were "drawn" into the event, committed as part of a team.   How could they not go forward?   Who would be the first to say "no?"

S. L. A. Marshall, chief U.S. Army combat historian during World War II and the Korean War, wrote, "'The touch of the elbow' provided a subtle, but solid, form of mental relief in a situation that the men, themselves, could not control. Man is a gregarious animal.   He wants company.   In his hour of greatest danger his herd instinct drives him towards his fellows.   It is a source of comfort to him to be close to other men; it makes danger more endurable."

Union soldier, E. L. Marsh, Iowa volunteers, seconded this observation: "The man who can go out alone and fight against overwhelming odds is very rare, and for every one such there are thousands who can 'touch the elbow' and go forward to what seems almost certain death."

The innate urge of soldiers to work closely together, however, caused men to bunch up at times when it was more prudent to spread out in order to provide proper coverage or to simply present smaller targets to the enemy. [210]

But if shoulder-to-shoulder formations could inspire a regiment to go on, the breakup of these formations could just as easily ruin the attack.   Breaking an assault line represented the fracturing of that bond that molded soldiers into a truly cohesive unit.   The collective will of the group was destroyed.   With this condition, soldiers drifted towards making decisions as individuals again, sometimes more concerned with surviving than with the objective of the unit.

An incoherent formation was crippled in movement and unresponsive to orders.   Loss of discipline promoted a premature response.   It degraded the accuracy of fire and the unit lost firepower because of clumping men who blocked others' view of the enemy.   A formation in the process of disintegration was obvious to the enemy and became a tempting opportunity to exploit.

The Battle Begins

But all the drilling, all the preparedness, all the virtues instilled in training, and all the tactics would not guarantee the behavior of these gentle-faced sons of America for an introduction to combat. Training helped some, but that was merely a mechanical drill devoid of psychological preparation for the shocking sights of a genuine encounter. Mock experiences could not duplicate this condition.

The mental transition from citizen to warrior was, in itself, extraordinary. In civilian life most men operated in a non-confrontational existence. They evaded danger by successfully relying on avoidance behavior. Now, in a confined area and moving to the commands of others, they must shift to the aggressive, kill others, and suppress their ever-present urge for self-preservation.

For many, first-time encounters were almost never mild introductions to action or tangential to a main event unfolding nearby and away from danger. Most men were not "eased" into combat to experience the full fury of it in stages. It usually happened at an inopportune moment, more like a sacrificial commitment to salvage a desperate situation, or the uninitiated were simply victims of an unlucky placement in a column.

The most sensible way of engaging the enemy was to use seasoned troops to dampen the shock for the novices. Preference for placement of battle-tested units over inexperienced ones for an orderly commitment to battle, however, was almost never practical. Units at the head of a column were the first engaged regardless of battle experience.

For those that did have some advance warning, Confederate Maj. Gen. D. H. Hill, in an address to his troops, explained one desensitizing effect to the initial shock:

Many opportunities will be afforded to the cavalry to harass the enemy,

112

Lookout Mountain. *JW/CWAR*

cut off his supplies, drive in his pickets, &c. Those who have never been in battle will thus be enabled to enjoy the novel sensation of listening to the sound of hostile shot and shell, and those who have listened a great way off will be allowed to come some miles nearer, and compare the sensation caused by the distant cannonade with that produced by the rattle of musketry. [211]

For others less fortunate, initial encounters would involve exposure to all the elements that shocked the soul. Life-altering experiences were rapidly introduced and jammed into that one event. Real battlefields were cluttered with horrific sights of men and animals torn apart, smells of burning flesh, screams of wounded broadcasting their unnerving pleas through deafening gunfire, and scenes of friends in their death throes. Such experiences were forever branded into the memories of survivors. [Today's military prepares the uninitiated in great detail. For a comprehensive discussion on this subject see Appendices].

The peak of performance for uninitiated units, trained well in the drill, was usually just before the action began. In reacting to telltale warning cues of an impending engagement, the men's senses are fully aroused with regards to their surroundings. They are alert, assessing the unfolding situation, attentive to orders, and, at this point, have a high degree of unit cohesion. They move about according to prescribed drills.

At this stage most must have asked themselves "How will I react?" "Will I pass the test?" "What have I gotten myself into?" These young, soon to be old, men, fresh off the farms, out of the villages and cities, would be hurled into an unforgettable experience, shocking their senses to a new level.

It is hard to overstate the level of tension caused by the feeling immediately before every battle. The heightened level of mental activity translated into stress reactions. Physical symptoms of fear begin to appear. A study of the emotional shock in war noted that, "most soldiers on approaching the firing line, displayed uneasiness and apprehension by restlessness, irritability, artificial jubilancy or silence and withdrawal or by unusual perspiration, diarrhea and frequency of micturation (urination)."

Lt. Col. John Pegram, C. S. A., at Rich Mountain, July, 1861, reported:

> I had just gotten all the men up together and was about making my dispositions for the attack when Major Tyler came up and reported that during the march up the ridge one of the men in his fright had turned around and shot the first sergeant of one of the rear companies, which had caused nearly the whole of the company to run to the roar. He then said that the men were so intensely demoralized, that he considered it madness to attempt to do anything with them by leading them on to the attack. A mere glance at the frightened countenances around me convinced me that this distressing news was but too true, and it was confirmed by the opinion of the three or four company commanders around me. [212]

Lt. Col. W. T. Poague noted: "The most trying time is 'waiting to go in.' The silence before the coming battle is oppressive. Many mental and physical exhibitions will be noticed, and if the battle is on, the sight of the wounded men streaming back is disheartening." One modern day platoon leader, in the Falklands, thought that pre-contact uncertainty and apprehension were far more disturbing than fear experienced during it. [213]

Waiting to go in. *UI/CWP*

Most Civil War veterans echo the same descriptive theme regarding the stress of entry into battle. The following is a composite of different accounts from eyewitnesses and, by then, seasoned veterans, giving us detailed insight into the building tensions as these warriors marched towards the battlefield. Most, but not all, pertain to their experiences at the battle of Gettysburg. They are spliced together to give to the reader the soldiers' view of the surrounding environment, what their impressions were, and their revelations regarding their sobering experience as they were about to engage the enemy. All quotes are in their own powerful and riveting words. It begins with the following:

Circular issued by the headquarters, Army of the Potomac, June 30, 1863:

> The commanding general requests that previous to the engagement soon expected with the enemy, corps and all other commanding officers address their troops, explaining to them briefly the immense issues involved in the struggle. The enemy are on our soil. The whole country now looks anxiously to this army to deliver it from the presence of the foe. Our failure to do so will leave us no such welcome as the swelling of millions of hearts with pride and joy at our success would give to every soldier of this army. Homes, firesides, and domestic altars are involved. The army has fought well heretofore; it is believed that it will fight more desperately and bravely than ever if it is addressed in fitting terms.
>
> Corps and other commanders are authorized to order the instant death of any soldier who fails in his duty at this hour.
>
> By command of Major-General Meade:
>
> S. Williams,
Assistant Adjutant-General [214]

[A description, as viewed from the Confederate ranks, in preparation for battle by Allen C. Redwood, then serving in Heth's division, 3rd Corps, which opened the battle of Gettysburg on July 1st]:

> Usually we knew there must be trouble ahead, but not always how imminent it might be. The column would be marching as it had been doing for perhaps some days preceding, the fatigue, heat, dust, and general discomfort being far more insistent upon the thought of the men than any consideration of its military objective. Perhaps the pace may have been rather more hurried than usual for some miles, and a halt, for any reason, was most welcome to the footsore troops, who promptly proceeded to profit by every minute of it—lying down on the dusty grass by the roadside, easing the knapsack straps and belts, and perhaps snatching the opportunity for a short smoke (for which there had been no breath to spare previously) or for a moistening of parched throats from the canteen. [215]

[A description from the Union perspective as troops approached Gettysburg from the opposite direction on July 1st - Recollection by L.A. Smith, 1st Lieutenant, 136th N.Y. Infantry]:

> The march from Emmitsburg on the morning of July 1 was exceedingly nagging, as it was made in quick time. The distant booming of a cannon soon increased the heartbeat. The heavy Enfield rifle, accoutrements, knapsack, haversack and canteen were no longer burdensome. Tired limbs, blistered feet and sore muscles no longer absorbed our thought or drew upon the willpower; the whole man was changed as by magic; quickened and apparently refreshed to a degree not explainable, and hardly to be appreciated by those who have never experienced the wondrous power of a battle already begun, and towards which one is rapidly marching. [216]

[Allen C. Redwood, 55th Va.]:

> A mounted orderly comes riding back, picking his way through the recumbent ranks, and pretending indifference to the rough chaffing prescribed by custom in the infantry as the appropriate greeting for the man on horseback—good-natured on the whole, even if a little tinged with envy—or some general officer with his staff is seen going forward at a brisk trot through fields bordering the road, or maybe a battery of guns directing its course towards some eminence. It becomes apparent that the check ahead is not due to such ordinary causes as a stalled wagon or caisson or to the delay occasioned by some stream to be forded; the objective aspect of the situation begins to assert itself; the thought of present personal discomfort gives place to that of prospective peril, and a certain nervous tension pervades the ranks. [217]

[From the Union side, July 1st]:

> As soon as his corps took to the road, Howard [11th corps commander], some of his staff, and a small escort trotted on ahead. They followed the Emmitsburg road, the most direct route, riding much of the way in adjoining fields in order to pass the troops and vehicles of the First Corps that struggled along the rutted and muddy road....By 10:30 (Howard) had reached the high ground at the Peach Orchard. [218]

[View of Union Brigadier General John Gibbon, division commander, 2nd Corps, July 1st approaching Gettysburg from Taneytown, Md.]:

> Early in the afternoon, we could see way off in the air, beyond the Round Top, bursting shells and clouds of smoke and soon found the road

blocked up with baggage wagons driven to the rear by panic-stricken drivers who with the greatest difficulty could be induced to give up the road to our artillery and ambulances. We had finally to tear down the fences and force the drivers, with drawn pistols, to park the wagons in the fields. Clearing the road in this way, vehicles and artillery traveled in the road, whilst the infantry marched, when it could, in the open fields alongside. [219]

[Allen C. Redwood, 55th Va.]:

The troops in front are moving now, filing off to right or left, to take their allotted position in the line, or possibly beginning a flank movement; there may be no fight today after all—these things have happened before, without any serious coming of it....We are not in the confidence of the powers that be and know nothing of their machinations, however intimately these may concern our fortunes. We only know that we have 'no orders' as yet.

This condition of affairs may continue for hours or for minutes. Meanwhile, the best thing to do is to make ourselves as comfortable as possible—the philosophy of the seasoned soldier, in all circumstances— and take the chance of being permitted to remain so, and we shall be all better prepared for the work if it *does* come.

But, hello! Look yonder! The battery-men, who have been lounging about, are standing to their pieces now, and immediately become busy executing mysterious movements about the same, in the methodical fashion distinctive of their arm...A dense white stream of smoke leaps from the muzzle, and the crashing report strikes our ears a few seconds later, as the gunners step forward again...Another shot and another, and yet another, and the smoke thickens and we discern only vaguely the movements at the cannon—but the war-music has begun and we know the battle has opened....

Ah! There is a staff-officer talking in an animated tone to the brigade commander, motioning with his hand, while the other closely studies a folding map which has just been handed to him and which he presently returns, nodding the while to signify he understands what he is expected to do.

"Attention!"—but we are already on our feet in advance of the order, and most willingly leave the road, now growing momentarily more insalubrious, following the head of the column through fields of stubble or fallow or standing corn, the blades of which cut and the pollen irritates the moist skin. Or it may be through dense woodland, where nothing is visible a few yards distant, in which furious fighting may occur and many men fall with the opposing lines in close contact, yet entirely concealed from each other, the position of either being only conjectured by the smoke and the direction of the firing, as the bullets from the opposite side come rapping against the tree trunks and cutting twigs and leaves overhead.

Before this stage is reached, however, there may be numerous changes of direction, countermarching and the like to attain the position; long lines of battle require a good deal of space for deployment, and in the woods, especially, it is not easy to determine in advance just how much ground any command will occupy. In each case, however, at some stage, the troops are in line, and we may suppose them there, awaiting the attack or about to deliver it, as may be. [220]

A Union lieutenant recollected his impression as he approached Gettysburg:

Nothing escapes observation; every fence and field, the whole topography of the country, the expression on comrades' faces, the tone of command, all are indelibly stamped on mind and memory to a degree that time itself does not efface.

We were ordered to "double quick," first taking the side of the road, giving the right of way to the much needed artillery, then as the necessity for our presence upon the field of battle became pressing we took to the fields and over the fences.

Just as we came up the slope and passed over the brow of Cemetery Hill we saw an artilleryman killed. As he was carrying ammunition from the caisson a cannon ball passed to the right of our regiment and so close to the man that he whirled around and around and fell upon his face dead. The concussion killed him....

Wounded men and stragglers now began to pass to the rear, their numbers constantly increasing, including broken detachments of regiments enquiring for their commands. Among them we recognized men from our home who had gone out under a previous call for troops. As they passed by, they called out the names of neighbor friends who had been killed, wounded or taken prisoner....

General Doubleday rode up, made an enquiry and then rode rapidly back to the front. His horse was covered with foam and the flushed face of the General bespoke the tremendous strain under which he was laboring. [221]

[From the Confederate side, Lt. Colonel Freemantle, British observer with Longstreet's 1st Corps, gave his observation from the Chambersburg Pike, near Gettysburg, on July 1st]:

At 3 P. M. we began to meet wounded men coming to the rear, and the number of these soon increased most rapidly, some hobbling alone, others on stretchers carried by the ambulance corps, and others in the ambulance wagons. Many of the latter were stripped nearly naked, and displayed very bad wounds. This spectacle, so revolting to a person unaccustomed to such sights, produced no impression whatever upon the advancing troops, who certainly go under fire with the most perfect nonchalance. They show no enthusiasm or excitement, but the most complete indifference. This is the effect of two years' almost uninterrupted fighting. [222]

The anticipation experienced by soldiers in the minutes before contact with the enemy was at its highest level and the agony of it, unbearable. One author graphically described the elevated excitement by members of the 20th Maine regiment about to receive the Confederate attack on Little Round Top at Gettysburg, July 2nd:

> These minutes of inactivity would be almost intolerable, but blind instinct would be getting their bodies ready—blood beating harder and faster through the arteries; lungs seeming to dilate deep down, reaching for more oxygen; stomach and intestines shrinking and stopping all movement; and tension rising to the point where it could shake a man like the passage of a powerful electric current. When it came, any kind of action would be a relief—and the reaction would be explosive. [223]

[Allen C. Redwood, 55th Va.]:

> It is perhaps the most ominous moment of all when the command is heard "Load at will—load!" followed by the ringing of rammers in the barrels and the clicking of gun-locks…. [Muzzleloaders have] a strange quick jar upon the ear, the dry metallic snapping running along the line when it came to "prime," and each man realized that when next heard it will be with no uncertain sound and closely followed by the command, "Fire!" [224]

A Confederate officer described the power of that one word, "Fire!," at the battle of Sailor's Creek, April, 1865:

> The Federal infantry had crossed the creek and were now coming up the slope in two lines of battle. I stepped in front of my line and passed from end to end, impressing upon my men that no one must fire his musket until I so ordered; that when I said "*ready*" they must all rise, kneeling on the right knee; that when I said "*aim*" they must all aim about the knees of the advancing line; that when I said "*fire*" they must all fire together, and that it was all-important they should follow these directions exactly, and obey, implicitly and instantly, any other instructions or orders I might give.
> …My memory records no musket shot on either side up to this time, our skirmishers having retired upon the main line without firing. The enemy showed no disposition to break into the charge, but continued to

advance in the same measured and even hesitating manner, and I allowed them to approach very close—I should be afraid to say just how close—before retiring behind my men, who, as before stated, were lying down.

I had continued to walk along their front for the very purpose of preventing them from opening fire; but now I stepped through the line and stationing myself about the middle of it, called out my orders deliberately—everything being in full sight of both parties, and the enemy, as I have every reason to believe, hearing every word. "*Ready!*" To my great relief, the men rose, all together, like a piece of mechanism, kneeling on their right knees and their faces set with an expression that meant—everything. "*Aim!*" The musket barrels fell to an almost perfect horizontal line leveled about the knees of the advancing front line. "*Fire!*"

I have never seen such an effect, physical and moral, produced by the utterance of one word. The enemy seemed to have been totally unprepared for it, and, as the sequel showed, my own men scarcely less so. The earth appeared to have swallowed up the first line of the Federal force in our front. There was a rattling supplement to the volley and the second line wavered and broke. [225]

Beyond the first shot

Once the first ordered shot was fired, spirits would rise to their peak. It provided instant relief to the tense atmosphere that built up during the pre-battle phase. Most had wanted the initial stage over with to dispel the suspense and uncertainty. It was more comfortable to operate when the battle settled down to a rhythm of action so the men could proceed with assigned tasks.

The business at hand displaced the time to think about fear. Lt. Col. W. T. Poague, Confederate artillery battalion commander at Gettysburg, reminisced on the robotic work of Southern cannoneers during the bombardment preceding Pickett's Charge:

> The roar of our guns was terrific. The explosion of the Federal shells, with a different sound, added to the tumult. In the midst of it our officers and men engaged were busy with their work, pausing only to give a cheer at the sight of an exploding caisson of the Federals. The work went on mechanically. Few orders were given and those had to be shouted. [226]

However, even then, loss of some control over the men, especially infantrymen, began to enter the picture. Isolated by smoke and confusion, soldiers were removed from the close scrutiny of their leadership. With this "freedom" they could fall back to their own devices in order to cope with the situation.

Precision and discipline could turn to sluggishness and disorder at the blink of an eye. The difficulty in preserving discipline in combat was described by a member of the 9th New York at Antietam:

> It is astonishing how soon, and by what slight causes, regularity of formation and movement are lost in actual battle. Disintegration begins with the first shot. To the book-soldier, all order seems destroyed, months of drill apparently going for nothing in a few minutes.
>
> The truth is, when bullets are whacking against tree-trunks and solid shot are cracking skulls like egg-shells, the consuming passion in the breast of the average man is to get out of the way. Between the physical fear of going forward and the moral fear of turning back, there is a predicament of exceptional awkwardness from which a hidden hole in the ground would be a wonderfully welcome outlet. [227]

The method of firing in a battle line helped play a role in steadying troops. General Orders No. 3, Hdqtrs., Army of the Mississippi, 326 stated:

> In the beginning of a battle, except by troops deployed as skirmishers, the fire by file will be avoided; it excites the men and renders their subsequent control difficult; fire by wing or company should be resorted to instead. During the battle the officers and non-commissioned officers must keep the men in the ranks, enforce obedience, and encourage and stimulate them, if necessary. [228]

Perhaps it hadn't crossed their minds or maybe it was too painful to contemplate, but no recruit, at first, really thought of their comrades as being killed or wounded in battle. It was less painful for them to imagine scenes of slain men on a field more so as anonymous beings and unfortunate casualties.

But seeing death's clasp was inevitable. It was the first sight of death which branded its deepest and everlasting impression into their memories. Many described the emotional sting of witnessing the "Great Unpleasantness" firsthand and the harsh initiation to their first glimpse of death. In describing Beaver Dam Creek, 1862, one Confederate

Goodbye. ACR/*B & L*

soldier wrote:

> It was at this point that, for the first time, I saw a man killed in battle. We were standing to arms awaiting orders to advance; another regiment of the brigade was supporting us a short distance to the rear—the Sixtieth Virginia….A shell plowed the crest of the elevation in front, and our line made a profound obeisance as it passed over; it seemed as if it must clear us but about reach the Sixtieth, and as I ducked I glanced back that way and witnessed its effects in their ranks.
>
> The body of a stalwart young fellow suddenly disappeared, and on the ground where he had stood was a confused mass of quivering limbs which presently lay still—the same shell, as I learned afterward, carried away the top of a man's head in our own regiment. [229]

First Phase of Battle

The initial phase of a battle was an all-important moment. It involved a flurry of activities: soldiers, animals and equipment prepared for action. Commanders at every level sought to position their men in line with adjacent units and exploit any terrain features available. They arranged fields of fire, positioned artillery,

Preparing defenses at the Wilderness. EF/*LICW*

ordered the removal of fences or trees, the building of breastworks, and the readying of weapons for the pending action. Preparation included inspiring words of advice or practical instructions to the waiting men.

The first phase often determined how the men would hold together for the duration of the action. Regardless of whether men were novices or veterans, going into action was the most emotional, unsteady, and frightening period of the soldiers' experience. A Virginia soldier described his experience at Gettysburg:

> [Under fire] the line soon loses all semblance of regular formation; the companies have become merely groups of men, loading and firing and taking advantage of any accident of ground—natural depression, tree, rock, or even a pile of fence rails that will give protection. But if the soldier is about where he belongs—to the right or left of the regimental colors, according to the normal place of his company in line—he feels reasonably sure of resuming formation whenever the command may come to "cease firing" and to "dress on colors" preparatory to an advance or charge. [230]

Breakdown of the drill occurred soon into the fray. Men fought with different levels of intensity and resolve. Attacking, especially, took exceedingly more courage than defending. In moving an unprotected line towards the defender's stronghold, lines were often broken up by obstacles accompanied by loss of connective control. Obstacles also gave men refuge. Naturally, they took cover in sunken roads, ravines, outcroppings of rocks, etc., sometimes at the risk of losing sight of their goal.

Frequent halts in an attack to reform were particularly dangerous and potentially catastrophic. Historian S.L.A. Marshall described the unplanned mechanisms that plagued all commanders and disrupted plans during an attack: "Once halted, even if there has been no damage, the line never moves as strongly or as willingly again. After three or four such fruitless delays, men become morally spent rather than physically rested. All impetus is lost and the attack might be better called off." [231]

Unanticipated changes in direction could also destroy momentum and derange plans. Changing course upset the rhythm and commitment established at the beginning. A change in tempo only magnified the uncertainty. This was further aggravated by seeing puzzling movements of friendly troops from adjacent units going to the rear, raising questions as to what was happening.

When the attack was fully underway, various levels of enthusiasm were revealed in the progressively growing non-linear shape of the once well-dressed line that formed at the beginning of the advance.

At the battle of Pittsburg Landing, or Shiloh, in 1862, Union Col. William Smith, commanding the 14th Brigade reported:

> The enemy soon yielded, when a running fight commenced, which extended for about one mile to our front, where we captured a battery

and shot the horses and many of the cannoneers. Owing to the obstructed nature of the ground, the enthusiastic courage of the majority of our men, the laggard discharge of their duty by many, and the disgraceful cowardice of some, our line had been transformed into a column of attack, representing the various grades of courage from reckless daring to ignominious fear. [232]

Rufus Dawes, 6th Wisconsin Infantry, described what an assault really looked like:

Any correct picture of this charge would represent a V-shaped crowd of men with the colors at the advance point, moving firmly and hurriedly forward, while the whole field behind is streaming with men who had been shot, and who are struggling to the rear or sinking in death upon the ground. The only commands I gave, as we advanced, were, "Align on the colors! Close up on that color! Close up on that color!" The regiment was being broken up so that this order alone could hold the body together. [233]

Anxiety

One product of battle was anxiety. Lurking in the background of all soldiers' minds was an immediate and an unpleasant feeling of loneliness. The anxiety produced from this sense of isolation was due primarily from reduced visibility caused by battle smoke or staying low to avoid getting shot. In *Infantry in Battle*, there is a description regarding the sense of isolation: "A soldier, pinned to the ground by hostile fire, with no form of activity to divert his thought from the whistling flails of lead that lash the ground about him, soon develops an overwhelming sense of inferiority. He feels alone and deserted. He feels unable to protect himself." "The longer the feelings of isolation and confusion lasted," observed historian, Joanna Burke, "the less likely it was that anyone would act aggressively." [234]

From the beginning of a battle, the willingness to fight became unstable. Levels increased or decreased by consciously or unconsciously absorbing information from surrounding events. Positive sights and sounds buoyed up men's spirits; seeing the power in one's own battle line provided reassurance and stimulated the confidence in a probable victory; hearing that reinforcements were on the way was comforting; the sound of friendly fire along the line was a welcomed aid in combating helplessness.

Conversely, the fracturing of a disciplined line could be caused by any number of negative sights or sounds manifested in the heat of battle. Witnessing the loss of a leader or cherished member of the unit ruffled spirits. Hearing the insecure confidence betrayed by the quivering voice of an officer relaying an order could

Under fire at Chancellorsville. WLS/*B & L*

shatter confidence.

A weak-willed shout from men in the ranks also dampened enthusiasm. Col. Morgan L. Smith, 8th Missouri Infantry, commanding brigade, in the advance upon and siege of Corinth in 1862 said, "An attempt was made…to drive us from the hill. A charge was made and an attempt to cheer by many voices, but the cheer was too feminine and seemed to say, 'Men, we don't want to fight you, but would like to frighten you off that hill.'" [235]

Perceptions, whether correct or not, such as believing the enemy was gaining control, or viewing the routine re-positioning of skirmishers from the front to the rear could upset discipline. When cohesion disappeared it was quite natural to continue firing either against the directives of the colonel or, at least, without his encouragement.

Federal General John Gibbon once testified in Washington on the influence of combat upon the discipline of soldiers:

> I am satisfied that if I had been able to get these men (to the left of his division) to do what I wanted, we would have captured a great many more [Confederates] than we did.
>
> **Question.** What was the difficulty?
>
> **Answer.** It was the want of proper discipline. Men get very much excited in battle; they are yelling, halloing, shooting, and unless they are very well drilled and disciplined, they do not wait for the orders of their colonels.
>
> **Question.** In the heat of the battle can a commanding officer have much control over his men?

Answer. Not after the men become thoroughly engaged. But if men are well disciplined and accustomed to listen implicitly to the voice of their officers they can have an immense influence over them, if they (officers) stand by them and direct them. [236]

The degree or speed to which a unit lost its fighting discipline was determined chiefly by the unit's distance to the enemy. Proximity bred fear and excitement which was restrained only by the imagination of each soldier. Besides that, units would move to and fro without commands to do so. Alignments would deteriorate and the line would take on, more or less, the characteristics of a skirmish line. With the decrease in cohesion, the ability to command was lost accordingly.

Men would bunch up or fight and take action independently of others. Each part of the line interpreted the problem differently and some sought to remedy the situation while disregarding the unit as a whole. "In the 80th N.Y., [at Gettysburg on July 3rd]... a color bearer jumped up on some stones, and waved his flag at the advancing lines, shouting for them to come on. All the men then stood up, and some of them started shooting, and had to be told to hold their fire until the Johnnies got within decent range."

Lieutenant Samuel B. McIntyre, 111th, N.Y. wrote: "We reserved our fire [near 12th N.J. and Brien Farm] until their last lines were within close firing distance. Thomas Geer of my company (A) with one or two others, could not be restrained, and went off to the right and fired down the lane."

When a regiment engaged at close range, it was not unusual to lose maneuverability by shunning the mechanical movements learned from training and simply stand in place and fire away until ammunition was expended. With even a moderate loss of discipline, it was hard to stop the action until the men decided it was time to do so.

Here, commanders must realize they were no longer in control of the situation. Orders issued from a rear command post were practically useless. The action had a life of its own and troops were unresponsive to commands   When this happened, unit cohesion had disintegrated. In the process, the regiment had been converted from a force programmed to respond to the orders of its leader to one in which the will to fight was tempered with self-preservation interests of the individual. It was at this stage the urge to fight or flee was strongest. [237]

Fight or Flight

Cowards die a thousand deaths; brave men die but once, and conquer though they die. [238]

Fight or flight? For those engaged in combat, the answer to this question

126

depended on an individual's self-discipline, state of morale, sense of duty, concern for the stigma attached to those abandoning their comrades at a crucial moment, and, perhaps most importantly, devotion to fellow soldiers.

For those reacting to their first shock of battle it was not uncommon in the Civil War to let blind panic take over. At this stage there was no cohesion nor did the unit exist as a recognizable force. It usually began with individuals breaking, followed by small groups building into larger ones. Those that remained on the line, reduced in numbers, eventually joined in until a stampede ensued. After all, in hopeless situations, the lives of the most courageous would only be wasted by remaining behind and continuing the fight. While cavalry seemed the most ready to rally, they were more apt to breaking. Artillerymen were burdened with the shame of losing their guns as a motive to stay united and remain in the fight. [239]

Bull Run is a good example of a stampede in action. Most soldiers fled in panic and, in the process, saved themselves for another day. As a result, only 10% of the regiments suffered. The rest had no killed, wounded, or captured. [240]

In the Seven Days' battles Confederate Maj. Gen. Daniel H. Hill spoke of the Federal retreat:

> So far as I can learn none of our troops drew trigger, except McLaws' division, mine, and a portion of Huger's. Notwithstanding the tremendous odds against us and the blundering management of the battle we inflicted heavy loss upon the Yankees.
>
> They retreated in the night, leaving their dead unburied, their wounded on the ground, three pieces of artillery abandoned, and thousands of superior rifles thrown away. None of their previous retreats exhibited such unmistakable signs of rout and demoralization. The wheat fields about Shirley were all trampled down by the frightened herd, too impatient to follow the road. Arms, accouterments, knapsacks, overcoats, and clothing of every description were wildly strewn on the road-side, in the woods, and in the field. Numerous wagons and ambulances were found stuck in the mud, typical of Yankee progress in war. [241]

Fleeing, of course, was not an option for soldiers to decide as individuals. It was a decision for their leaders to remain or withdraw from the battlefield. It is always implied that commanders knew more what was going on in the battle line than those that were in it and, therefore, they could make the best choices. To trust a leader's decision in this regard, however, was a supremely weighty acquiescence in allowing others to determine one's destiny while overcoming the self-preservation instincts as individuals. That leaders determined the fate of so many, sometimes proved to be an injudicious waste of lives. Poor judgment or poor leadership happened too often and to too many.

Taking flight without orders to do so was a serious action and culturally unacceptable. Civilian society viewed the war as necessary for noble and glorious reasons. Flight represented cowardice. It was a failure of character and moral weakness in those unable to control their fears.

Besides, flight was merely a temporary solution to an immediate problem that would come back to haunt those that escaped their duty. There was nothing worse than losing respect and being labeled a coward by the men that remained on the field who were forced into facing more danger and more risk with fewer men.

Major Osborn, Union artillerist, witnessed the premature flight of one battery:

> I…saw [a] battery with all the men mounted on the ammunition chests going at full speed, the horses running down the Baltimore Pike, the drivers whipping their horses at every jump. I never saw the battery again, and as it did not belong to my command, I did not report it to its proper superiors. Doubtless, the Captain reported to the commander of the Reserve Artillery that he was in the hottest of the fight and that he and all his men were heroes. At all events, the giant monument on Cemetery Hill stands to the credit of that battery. [242]

World War II General George Patton made no bones about using peer pressure to subdue the instinct to flee:

> The greatest weapon against the so-called "battle fatigue" is ridicule. If soldiers would realize that a large proportion of men allegedly suffering from battle fatigue are really using an easy way out, they would be less sympathetic. Any man who says he has battle fatigue is avoiding danger and forcing on those who have more hardihood than himself the obligation of meeting it. If soldiers would make fun of those who begin to show battle fatigue, they would prevent its spread, and also save the man who allows himself to malinger by this means from an after-life of humiliation and regret. [243]

Those guilty of fleeing might overcome their disgrace by performing more heroic actions later, thereby cancelling out their misdeeds. If not, the stigma remained permanent for those that settled back in their communities to work alongside men that had witnessed their indecorous actions. Peer pressure is what propelled many to choose fight over flight, to risk death again and again, and to avoid censure.

The only acceptable excuses for a combat soldier not to fight were death, a wound, or an incapacitating injury or illness. There was another choice, however, between fight or flight. It was a choice that would avoid the stigma of flight and still maintain the appearance that there was involvement. Some soldiers remained in the fray but did not perform with the same commitment as others. Experienced soldiers, for example, not eager to make targets of themselves, simply remained under cover and stayed there.

Others may have used false reasons to go to safer zones in the rear. Wasting ammunition to deplete supplies in order to leave the field was one technique. At

Gettysburg, William H. McCartney, First Massachusetts Battery, reported that from his battery, "...I caused to be collected, from a piece of woods directly in the rear of the ground which had been occupied by said...battery, 48 rounds of 3-inch projectiles, perfect; 22 rounds having been found near the position which had been occupied by one limber." [244]

Some fled the field under the guise of helping wounded to the rear. Part of Confederate Gen. Beauregard's Order No. 3 stated:

> Before and immediately after battle the roll of each company will be called, and absentees must strictly account for their absence from the ranks. To quit their standard on the battlefield, under fire, under the pretense of removing or aiding the wounded, will not be permitted; any one persisting in it will be shot on the spot, and whosoever shall be found to have quit the field or his regiment or company without authority will be regarded and proclaimed as a coward, and dealt with accordingly. [245]

Some used ingenious ways of shirking their duty. At Gettysburg, one musket was found on the field to have twenty-three rounds in it without being fired. Understandably, mistakes were made in the heat of the action where several unfired rounds were inadvertently rammed down the barrel, but not twenty-three.

Although just speculation, one possibility is that it appears whoever did this, was simply trying to look busy. Soldiers had loaded and fired their muzzleloaders hundreds of times. Repetitive use established where the ramrod stopped in the barrel during the loading process. A probable theory is that this soldier was in an attacking line. To escape danger, he couldn't simply walk slower than the others because of file-closers in the rear assigned to prod shirkers forward. Looking "busy" by continuously loading may have created the deceptive appearance that this man was standing there doing his duty and blended in with the action, while his battle line moved towards the enemy.

Beyond the individual's preference to fight or flee, other factors influenced this important decision. Coercive means were applied to help soldiers make the correct choice. At Stone's River, in 1862, Confederate Capt. Felix H. Robertson, Florida artilleryman, used his persuasive power to stop his men fleeing from the field:

> The contagion of flight had spread to the artillery, and it was with great difficulty that several pieces of artillery were brought away, owing to the drivers being frightened. In more than one instance I found it necessary to cock my revolver and level it in order to bring men to a realizing sense of their duty. [246]

At the same battle, Lt. Col. John G. Parkhurst, 9th Michigan Infantry, reported:

> On Wednesday morning, about two hours after the commencement of Wednesday's battle, I noticed many stragglers crossing the fields from

the direction of the right wing of our army, and sent out forces and brought them in, until I had from 100 to 200 collected, when I discovered several cavalrymen approaching with great speed from the direction of our front, and very soon discovered that a large cavalry force, together with infantry and a long transportation train, were in the most rapid retreat, throwing away their arms and accouterments, and many of them without hats or caps, and apparently in the most frightful state of mind, crying, "We are all lost."

I at once concluded it was a stampede of frightened soldiers, and before many had passed me I drew my regiment up in line of battle across the road, extending on either side, and ordered my men to fix bayonets, and to take the position of guard against cavalry. This was done with celerity, and with much difficulty. Without firing upon the frightened troops, I succeeded in checking their course, and ordered every man to face about. Within half an hour I had collected about 1,000 cavalrymen, seven pieces of artillery, and nearly two regiments of infantry. Among them was a brigadier-general. [247]

To prevent unauthorized flight, guards such as cavalrymen or provost guards were placed immediately to the rear of battle lines to either gather up and guard prisoners or prevent front line soldiers from prohibited movements. Their presence provided great assistance to unit commanders on the line who were too preoccupied with more immediate concerns. Guards insured that soldiers remained with their units, they prevented stressed soldiers from seeking safety on their own by bolting to the rear, and monitored those behind the lines to verify that their presence was authorized.

Soon after the battle of Gettysburg, the Provost-Martial-General, Marsena R. Patrick, complained to the Army of the Potomac's Assistant-Adjutant-General, Seth Williams, about the lack of control over the movement of men about the field:

> During the recent engagements, large numbers of soldiers were passed to the rear, not only by surgeons, but by commanding officers; without specifying place; consequently, they were scattered over the whole country in the rear of the line of battle. Large numbers of enlisted men were also found beyond the line of fire, in charge of pack mules, officers' horses, mess establishments, and company and regimental property, as well as guards of general officers, pioneer detachments, entirely unarmed, regimental bands, and field music, scattered all along the rear, all of which were on no duty whatever.
>
> I would respectfully suggest that all musicians be put on hospital duty, in order that others, on such duty, may be relieved; that pioneers be compelled to remain with their regiments; that personal guards, excepting such as are absolutely necessary, be ordered to the ranks, and that no enlisted man whatever be permitted to take charge of officers'

private property; that all company and regimental property be carried with the regimental baggage, and that all permits to fall to the rear from line of battle, in time of action, shall specify to what hospital.

Corps and division commanders should point out to their provost-marshals, respectively, their line of battle so soon as formed, that their guards may be deployed in rear, at proper distances, to check disorder, and, in a crisis, to be put in with the troops. With their respective reserves the provost-marshals should habitually be found. Provost-marshals should keep themselves acquainted as to the position of the hospitals of their commands, making frequent inspections of the same, to see that no stragglers and skulkers are gathered there. [248]

But even safeguards employed to prevent unauthorized movements could not maintain total control over soldiers and keep them from running. Kent Graham, in his work *Gettysburg: A Meditation on War and Values* described such occasions:

…Sometimes soldiers cannot be reached by any [influences.] Occasionally a man runs from the line, eyes wide and unfocused, and no amount of exhortation, cajoling, threats, or profanity can stop him. The officer may hit him full force with the flat of his sword—but he could also slice off a hand and have the same non-effect. The soldier is in what was called "shell-shock" in World War I.

In World War II it was called "battle fatigue." A man may have been steady, even valorous, in all previous battles, and might be so again. But unreasoning fear takes control; the only instinct is to get away, either by running or by falling into a catatonic world.

File closers knew by experience that such men could not be turned, though no doubt many were struck, beaten, even shot in exasperation. It was known during World War II that *all* soldiers eventually reach that state, if subjected to continuous battle.

The nineteenth-century ideas of courage, character, and conscious will give way to the facts of modern war. Under the stress of constant combat, the soldier breaks down if he survives long enough. Death or shock: there is no third alternative for anyone—assuming no end to combat. Some will hold out longer than others: those are the ones we are interested in. [249]

Although keeping men steady during a fight was difficult, it was, nevertheless accomplished with most units, most of the time, experienced ones in particular. Kent Gramm's work also describes in detail the amount of encouragement needed to keep a unit intact during combat:

A running soldier cannot be stopped. In a Civil War infantry engagement…the officers would stand a couple of paces behind the firing line and constantly talk to the men…

When holes were shot through the line, these officers would encourage the men to close up, to stay in formation. Men under pressure would have two natural tendencies—and discipline in battle is meant to negate the natural tendencies, which are based on self-preservation.

One tendency is to bunch up, breaking the line's integrity. The bolder men tend to advance a step or two while firing; the less bold tend to edge in behind such men in clumps, partly protected by the body of the leader. The other tendency is to drift backward; unchecked, this could result in actually leaving the line for the rear.

These tendencies are rational, and can be neutralized by discipline, reason, threats, and all the other motivators of people in battle. It is in itself insane to stand in a line out in the open and trade bullets with a well-armed enemy; a gerbil would know better.

Human beings can be induced to do it for a number of reasons, in addition to killer instinct or death wish: shame at being seen as cowardly, for instance, a culturally induced phenomenon more effective, obviously, at some times and places than at others; hatred of the enemy; discipline inculcated by intense training; fear of punishment;...ideology— applicable to the volunteers of 1861; devotion to comrades; stupidity; mass psychological influences; sense of duty. [250]

Despite the difficulty in maintaining discipline, there are many examples where control held up under the most spectacular conditions. Lieutenant Anthony W. McDermott, 69th Pa. Volunteers commented on the enemy's discipline during Pickett's Charge: "When about two thirds of the field, that lay between the stone wall and the Emmitsburg pike, had been crossed, the enemy changed his direction in as good order, as when marching directly to the front, when within about 20 yards of us we received the command to fire..." [251]

Once close contact was made with the enemy, however, disintegration of discipline was the rule. It is easy to imagine the chaos in the final stages of an assault, especially in a large one like Pickett's advance on July 3rd. Near its climax, Confederate Major Charles Peyton, brigade commander replacement for General Garnett who was killed in the attack, wrote in his battle report:

We were now within about 75 paces of the wall, unsupported on the right and left, General Kemper being some 50 or 60 yards behind and to the right, and General Armistead coming up in our rear.

General Kemper's line was discovered to be lapping on ours, when, deeming it advisable to have the line extended on the right to prevent being flanked, a staff officer rode back to the general to request him to incline to the right. General Kemper not being present (perhaps wounded at the time), Captain [W.T.] Fry, of his staff, immediately began his exertions to carry out the request, but, in consequence of the eagerness of the men in pressing forward, it was impossible to have the order carried out. [252]

Stabilizing Broken Morale

The bravest thing you can do when you are not brave is to profess courage and act accordingly. Corra Harris

Once shattered, a positive state of morale was difficult to maintain or improve in any given situation. It could be done, however, by using a variety of methods to transform a chaotic scene to one of steadfastness. At Gettysburg, Col. James E. Mallon, Forty-second New York Infantry, tried to stabilize retreating units of the Union 3rd Corps on July 2nd. "At this time," Mallon reported, "all the troops to the front were precipitately retiring in great disorder. To avoid the enfilading effect of the fire, which was now rapidly thinning the ranks; to infuse confidence in the hearts of those who among those retreating might have some manhood left; to present a disciplined, unwavering front toward the rapidly approaching and confident enemy, the two regiments formed line." [253]

The presence of senior commanders, visibly sharing dangers with their troops, was also important. Leaders were there to help rally a shaken unit or provide intelligent direction when actions were desperate. Many times they were

Being seen at the front. LP/LOC

perilously close to enemy fire, deliberately exposing themselves for effect. Doing so supplied confidence, produced upbeat feelings, and gave the sense that leaders cared for the well-being of the men.

One Union soldier, advancing on Fort Donelson, Tennessee, exclaimed his new-found inspiration when he saw his commander, General C.F. Smith, riding unruffled through the storm of Confederate minie balls: "I was scared to death, but I saw the old man's white mustache over his shoulder, and went on." [254]

It is the officers' responsibility to be the steadying influence during combat. It is the leader who establishes the character of the unit. His hallmark of excellence is revealed in his men's willingness to follow orders. If the men respected their leader as a strong and capable role model, they feel less anxiety, more secure, and willing to react to their leader's entreaties. [Today, this is known as "command climate."] [255]

Stonewall Jackson epitomizes what leadership can do to influence soldiers on the brink of defeat. Dr. Hunter McGuire, medical director, in an address once stated:

> At Malvern Hill, when a portion of our army was beaten and to some extent demoralized, Hill and Ewell and Early came to tell him that they could make no resistance if McClellan attacked them in the morning. It was difficult to wake General Jackson, as he was exhausted and very sound asleep. I tried it myself, and after many efforts, partly succeeded. When he was made to understand what was wanted he said: "McClellan and his army will be gone by daylight," and went to sleep again. The generals thought him mad, but the prediction was true.
>
> ...The story illustrates two of the greatest and most distinguishing traits and powers of Jackson as a general: he did not know what demoralization meant, and he never failed to know just what his adversary thought and felt and proposed to do. In the present instance, not only did all that Jackson said and implied turn out to be true, that McClellan was thinking only of escape, and never dreamed of viewing the battle of Malvern Hill in any other aspect, but in an incredibly short time our army had recovered its tone and had come to take the same view of the matter. [256]

To prevent collapsing morale amidst the turmoil, officers presented a serene image of nonchalance in front of their men, performed with composure, issued orders with authority, and responded with an air of self-confidence in overturning the disappointments and setbacks that led to defeat and converted desperate situations into victory.

Paul Fussell, author and World War II veteran, wrote of leaders using the "game face" to exemplify confidence:

> The whole trick for the officer is to seem what you would be, and the formula for dealing with fear is ultimately rhetorical and theatrical: regardless of your actual feelings, you must simulate a carriage which

will affect your audience as fearless, in the hope that you will be imitated or, at least, not be the occasion of spreading panic. [257]

For Civil War artillery officers to operate in battle, it required extraordinary mental discipline and concentration. Their definition of courage required them to face enemy fire unperturbed.

Lt. Bayard Wilkeson holding his battery in position. AW/*B & L*

Major Thomas Osborn, Union artillery brigade commander, described what it took to perform at Gettysburg during Pickett's Charge on July 3rd:

> This terrific artillery battle, which all knew was the immediate forerunner of victory or defeat, was [exceptionally pressing to the human condition]…During such time, the force of will which an officer must bring to bear upon himself in order not only to control his men but also govern himself, is wonderful. He must by sheer force of will shut up every impulse of his nature, except that of controlling the officers and men subject to his command. He must discard all care of his personal safety and even his own life. The most difficult person to control is always himself. [258]

Osborn also shared an introspective and personal experience that disclosed his great respect and importance for self-control in battle:

While the artillery fire was still at its highest, [Captain Wadsworth, a son of General Wadsworth] came to me with some directions and to make some inquiries for headquarters. I was at the moment on a nice horse thoroughly accustomed to me. His horse was the same. We halted close together in the midst of the batteries, the horses headed in the opposite directions and our faces near together. Neither horse flinched. The forelegs of each horse were in line with the hind legs of the other, and we stood broadside to the enemy fire.

While we were talking, a percussion shell struck the ground directly under the horses and exploded. The momentum of the shell carried the fragments along so that neither horse was struck nor did neither horse move. When the shell exploded, I was in complete control of my nerves and did not move a muscle of my body or my face. Neither did Wadsworth, but *I dropped my eyes to the ground where the shell exploded, and Wadsworth did not* [italics added].

I never quite forgave myself for looking down when that shell exploded under us. I do not believe that there was a man in the entire army, save Captain Wadsworth, who could have a ten pound shell explode under him without looking where it struck. [Maj. Osborn's shame is hardly unforgivable.] [259]

Subordinates observed their officers, scrutinizing them to detect the slightest "crack" in their composure. When Confederate Maj. Robert Stiles was reviewing the mismanagement of the battle at Malvern Hill with Lieutenant-colonel Brandon, 21st Mississippi, Brandon responded with deep dissatisfaction, mortification and rage:

> "Oh! it is not mismanagement that hurts me, sir; it is cowardice—the disgraceful cowardice of our officers and men."

I was astounded, and protested that I saw nothing of this, when he broke out again:

> "Saw nothing of this, sir? Why, I saw nothing else! There is General ---,"

...mentioning a man I never heard mentioned on any other occasion save with admiration for his courage and devotion.

> Why, sir, with my own eyes I saw him perceptibly quicken his pace under fire and that, right before the men. And I saw him visibly incline his head, sir, and that right in the presence of the men. He ought to be shot to death for cowardice. [260]

136

Courageous deeds which disregarded danger were, of course, life-threatening. There are countless examples of leaders, however, manipulating soldiers' morale by risking their lives to strengthen fighting spirit. The presence of senior officers in combat, leading the charge or riding the lines during dangerous bombardments inspired the men to rally and maintain discipline. The absence of leaders taking risks at the front, likewise, could completely dampen the spirits of troops.

Morale was also buoyed by other visual sights. Batteries interspersed down a battle line was a welcome psychological relief for soldiers. It maintained a protective feeling for infantry soldiers, particularly inexperienced ones, and they gained enormous encouragement from it.

Gen. Howard rallying his troops at Chancellorsville. *RFZ/B & L*

At the beginning of the war, Union Gen. Irvin McDowell wanted more artillery in his unskilled army to instill confidence in his troops. General Sherman said later: "In the early stages of the war the field-guns often bore the proportion of six to a thousand men; but toward the close of the war, one gun, or at most two, to a thousand men, was deemed enough." [261]

Besides visual support gained from friendly artillery, soldiers also liked the sound of their own cannons. Friendly artillery fire signaled that something was being done in response to the enemy's actions. This sound effect was so important, commanders were willing to waste precious artillery ammunition in order to reassure troops manning the battle line.

The confidence-building value produced was called upon on more than one occasion at Gettysburg. From Little Round Top on July 2nd, Union guns were fired to preserve morale even though their barrels could not be depressed enough to hit the attackers approaching the heights.

But using artillery for this purpose bore no controversy like it would on July 3rd which sparked the famous argument between Gen. George Meade's chief-of-artillery, Gen. Hunt, and 2nd corps commander, Gen. Hancock. In short, when the great cannonade began, Hunt wanted a muted response by Union artillery to

Chickahominy. WW/*LICW*

save the limited supply of on-hand ammunition for killing enemy infantrymen should an attack take place. Hancock, on the other hand, wanted to blast away with a full response from the beginning simply to reassure his waiting infantry.

Here, Hancock was willing to trade his firepower for the immediate benefit of boosting the confidence and steadfastness in his men. With his command being punished by this epic bombardment, he saw the need to stabilize the morale of his men for what was likely to come.

There were other ways used to preserve or stabilize morale of soldiers engaged in combat. Tactics employed such as the judicious use of reserves was one of the most effective ways to influence confidence. Skilled commanders had an innate feel for judging the "ripeness" of a battle and when to withhold reserve forces and, at the right moment, commit them to action.

Timing for feeding reserves into the fight was an important morale booster to prevent defeat or exploit an advantage. Reserves were needed when elements in the line had reached a stage of near panic, to fill a hole in the line, to attack an enemy flank, or to reinforce or replace units. Feeding too many onto the field interfered by getting in the way of others' loading and firing. On the other hand, not enough men on the field could sway the battle in favor of the opponents just from the appearance of being overwhelmed by the enemy, resulting in a stampede.

Diversions

Maintaining strict control of a unit once battle action began was a difficult task despite the active participation of unit officers. Sometimes training skills provided enough discipline to keep men on the battle line and obedient to orders. But once the intensity of the fight increased, it became more difficult to maintain control. It defied an effective solution and perplexed many commanders on Civil War battlefields.

There were a number of diversions, however, which focused troops' mental and physical resources on actions to hold discipline and helped keep men alive. Diversions forced men to concentrate on their work at hand and short-circuited the effects of fear.

Diversions were both natural and contrived. Combat, itself, was a primary natural diversion. A Confederate artilleryman noted:

> ...Once engaged, the sense of duty and the absorption of occupation will greatly overcome every other sensation. Every man has his duty to do, and if he does it he will have little time to think of anything else. No place can be considered safe. In this action [Gettysburg, July 3rd], a man was standing behind a tree near our battalion, safe from direct fire. But a passing shell exploded just as it passed; the fragments struck him and tossed his dead body out. The sight reassured those who were in the open. [262]

Soldiers in combat, rather than spending most of the time dwelling on their mortality, concentrated by listening intently to discern commands garbled by noise and being alert to threats surrounding them. Moving in formation, in particular, needed a high level of attentiveness, especially complex moves such as changes of direction, crossing terrain impeded with obstacles, or over uneven ground.

Detailed attention was needed to safely operate weapons and perform the proper sequence of movements. This was amidst the gunfire of others only inches away. In firing, those in the rear rank had to have the muzzles of their weapons beyond the faces of the front rank. They aimed with limited fields of fire, between the heads of the two men in the front rank. When triggers were pulled, those in the front were jarred by the deafening explosion and searing flame at ear level.

One modern day writer described it as "muskets slamming all around you, smoke in your eyes. Biting cartridges dried out your mouth and throat and left your teeth and tongue gritty and hating each other. At the end, your shoulder might be bruised black, your head ached and rang, your voice was a croak, and your thirst was intolerable." [263]

[Confederate Allen C. Redwood] talks about this experience at Gettysburg:

Once engaged, the soldier's attention is too much taken up with delivering his fire effectively to heed to much else—it is hard work and hot work....and extremely dirty work withal. The lips become caked with powder-grime from biting the twist of cartridges, and after one or two rounds the hands are blackened and smeared from handling the rammer; the sweat streams down and has to be cleared from the eyes in order to see the sights of the rifle, and the grime is transferred from the hands to face....

[In the process of attacking Biddle's brigade on McPherson's Ridge, the rate of fire from the men in the 47th N.C. Infantry was slowed when their sweaty hands slipped on the ramrods of their muskets as they forced down the cartridges. To overcome this, many jammed their rammers against the ground and rocks.] [264]

Close quarters. WH/*B & L*

In situations where no positive movements were performed to draw the concentration of the men, regimental commanders resorted to contrived methods of retaining the focus of their unit. They might have preoccupied their attention mentally with shouted orders and phrases of inspiration, invoked a pep talk to buoy their spirits, or resorted to a physical solution such as drilling the men in the manual of arms.

Even though drilling during combat increased the exposure of men to more danger, a commander could take his men's minds off their hazardous circumstances by performing actions incompatible with the situation. Such distractions kept men on the line and provided some relief.

Col. Henry Morrow, 24th Michigan Infantry, under artillery fire at

Fredericksburg, realized his men, now in their first battle, could not bear the inaction without the chance to fight back. To overcome this, he brought his regiment to attention and drilled them in the manual of arms.

In another example, Union Brig. Gen. Alexander Hays, 2nd Corps, during the July 3rd cannonade at Gettysburg, diverted the minds of his troops' dangerous predicament by suddenly appearing and ordering his men to gather all the abandoned muskets, clean them, and load them for use. When the Confederate infantrymen were approaching the Emmitsburg Road, Hays drilled some of his troops in the manual of arms to help subdue their "fight or flight" instincts. [265]

Shouting

Morale was stimulated by sound as well. Verbal encouragement reinforced resolve and helped sustain troops in combat. A simple thing like shouting was one seemingly insignificant example of how vocalization could aid military success to gain a victory.

There was nothing more encouraging to Union men, for example, than to hear thousands of their comrades shouting cheers of "huzzah's" up and down the lines or for Confederates to hear their distinct rebel yell.

Officers shouted basic instructions to adjust unit movements, prepare weapons, or any positive phrases to maintain confidence. Officers in an attack often shouted themselves hoarse to communicate above the sounds of tramping feet and the clanking and creaking of equipment shifting about the men as they moved forward. "Steady, boys," "Give 'em hell, boys!," "Load your musket," were yelled out even though these words might be unintelligible and drowned out by background noise. Inspirational exclamations were frequently used by leaders to coerce men forward. "For God and country!," "For your loved ones!," or similar appeals could be heard up and down the line. Officers on a defensive line shouted instructional orders such as "Aim for the knees!," or "Hold fire until the order is given!"

Shouting by troops, although more prevalent among inexperienced troops than veterans, was beneficial group therapy by validating unit cohesion. Whole units were encouraged to shout. The blaring chorus of hundreds of soldiers energized spirits to heightened levels while it deflated the sense of danger. In the Atlanta campaign of 1864, Lieut. Col. Samuel R. Mott, 57th Ohio Infantry, reported the great benefit shouting gave his men:

> Soon preparations were completed, and the bugle notes sounded "forward," With yells and shouts the enthusiastic troops went wildly over the field, under a terrible shower of lead, shot, and shell. I was instructed to hold my command at the foot of the hill to await further orders, but the war spirit so filled every breast that nothing was thought of but the occupation of the enemy's works on the crest of the hill; on and up the

line of battle moved fearlessly and bravely. [266]

At Manassas Gap, in pursuit of Lee's army after Gettysburg, Col. John S. Austin, 72nd N. Y. was ordered to charge the heights and drive off the enemy. In his report he stated:

> With a yell that would have done credit to a band of demons, our boys sprang to their feet and rushed upon the foe. The first and second heights were carried in the face of a severe fire, when the enemy opened from the opposite hill with a four-gun battery, and the men, who were now completely exhausted, were ordered to hold the position, of which they had so gallantly taken possession. [267]

There were also shouts that induced the opposite effect on the enemy. The sounds of determination in the form of Union soldiers' "huzzah's" or the spine-tingling rebel yells from an attacking formation unnerved many in the opposing force. Soldiers sometimes used foul language to divert their minds from a dangerous situation and strengthen their willpower. Captured Confederates told a Connecticut captain, John Deforest, "that they were not hurt much by the fact that his [Deforest's] men fired as they advanced, but they certainly were scared by the enemy's wild yelling and cursing." [268]

Humor

Surprisingly, soldiers immersed in battle still retained a sense of humor. They often laughed despite their surrounding misery. Humor, had a beneficial, even medicinal, effect on the mind. It cut the tension and created a calming effect on the men.

At Gettysburg, July 2nd, for example, the U.S. Regulars advanced towards Plum Run Valley from Little Round Top to meet the enemy head on. A lieutenant in the 14th U.S. focused on the work ahead. He left his customary place in the line and ran along the rear of the company yelling, "Give 'em h---, men! Give 'em h---!" The company commander, Capt. Chase commented, "Twice I ordered him to desist, telling him I was in command and to keep quiet. When we made the run across the marsh, this Lieutenant was particularly vociferous, swinging his sword, etc., and in the center of the marsh he fell and was covered with mud. His sword scabbard had gotten between his legs and tripped him. All who saw his misadventure laughed." [269]

Also on July 2nd, the 118th Pennsylvania waited for the enemy in a field east of the Emmitsburg Road. As Lafayette McLaws' Confederate division moved towards them, it flushed a frightened rabbit from the fields and towards the Pennsylvanians. The confused animal jumped into the men and "plunged his cold, sharp claws firmly into the neck of a soldier who lay flat near the edge of the regiment." The man, shocked by the surprised visitor jumped up shouting that he was a dead man, thinking he was shot through his neck. The eyewitnesses beamed with laughter as the embarrassed soldier disappeared into the battle line.[270]

In another case, some famished men of the 3rd Michigan found a windfall during the fight—honey-laden beehives in a nearby garden. During an attempt to harvest this treasure the bees attacked furiously, repeatedly stinging the men as they surrendered the quest by their quick retreat. An amused eyewitness, the Color Sgt., Daniel Crotty, later described the effect that the attacking swarm of bees caused the men to "turn such somersaulting on the ground as to put to shame a lot of Japanese acrobat performers in a circus ring." The still-famished victims were described as having "swollen heads and faces now resembling huge mortar shells." Crotty added, "So I think they will be content to hunt rebels after this, and leave their bees alone." [271]

Confederate Maj. Robert Stiles gives an unusual anecdote about a grievously wounded fellow officer:

> While a prisoner at Johnson's Island, in the spring of '65, I became much interested in one of my fellow-prisoners, a Major McDaniel, of Georgia. He did not at first strike one as an impressive man. Indeed, if I recollect rightly, he had somewhat of an impediment in his speech and was not inclined to talk much; but there was a peculiar pith and point and weight in what he did say, and those who knew him best seemed to regard him as a man of mark and to treat him with the greatest respect. The impression he made upon me was of simplicity and directness, good sense and good character, dignity, gravity, decorum. They told me this surprising story of him:
>
> He was seriously wounded at Gettysburg, and, of course, in the hospital. His friends who had been captured and were about to be marched off to prison, came in to bid him good-by; but he declared he would not be left behind, that he could and would go with them. Both his comrades and the Federal surgeons and nurses, who were kind and attentive, protested that this was absolutely out of the question—that he would die on the road.
>
> "Very good," said McDaniel, "I'll die then. I am certainly going, and if you don't bring a litter and put me on it and carry me, then I will simply get up and walk till I drop."
>
> Finally the surgeons yielded, saying that, in his condition, it would be as fatal to confine him forcibly in bed as to lift him out and attempt to transport him; that either course was certain death. So the litter was brought, he was placed upon it, his friends sadly took hold of the bearing poles and started, feeling that the marching column of prisoners was really McDaniel's funeral procession.
>
> The journey would have been trying enough, even for a sound, strong

man, but for one in McDaniel's condition it was simply fearful. Why he did not die they could not see, yet he did seem to grow weaker and weaker, until at last, as the column halted in a little Pennsylvania town and his bearers put the litter gently down in the shade, his eyes were closed, his face deadly pale, and the majority of those about him thought he was gone. The whole population was in the streets to see the Rebel prisoners go by, and some stared, with gaping curiosity, at the dead man on the stretcher.

His most intimate friend, Colonel Nesbit, stood nearest, keeping a sort of guard over him, and just as he made up his mind to examine and see if it was indeed all over, McDaniel opened his eyes, and beckoned feebly for Nesbit to come close to him. As he reached his side and bent over him, McDaniel took hold upon the lapel of Nesbit's coat and drew him yet closer down, until their faces well nigh touched, and then, with a great effort and in a voice scarcely audible, McDaniel whispered his name—"Nesbit!"

Nesbit says he confidently expected some last message for his family, or some tender farewell to his friends, when, with extreme difficulty, his supposed-to-be-dying friend, pointing with trembling finger, uttered just these words:

"Nesbit, old fellow! Did you ever see such an ungodly pair of ankles as that Dutch woman standing over there on that porch has got?"

Of course such a man could not be killed and would not die; and it was not a matter of surprise to me when, a few years later, he was elected Governor of Georgia by a hundred thousand majority. [272]

Music

Musical instruments were another source of audible comfort in times of stress. Besides the fact that drums and bugles were used as a vital tool to communicate commands or cadence, they, combined with other instruments, had an important role in broadcasting music to the troops. Their value is evidenced in the quantities procured in four years. Three of the many northern depots reported the purchase of 21,427 bugles, 14,858 trumpets, 37,496 drums,

Beating the long roll. WH/B & L

and 32,640 fifes. [273]

Beyond pure entertainment value, music was used as a powerful tool to influence soldiers. During battle, music buoyed spirits. Its soothing effects steadied nerves and helped create the appearance of an improved situation. Hearing a band playing the patriotic melodies of *Dixie* or *Battle Hymn* was a musical reminder of home and country. It raised determination to fight harder.

Music could also have an effect in stemming the retreat of nervous troops. In May, 1862, at the battle of Williamsburg, Va., Union Brig. Gen. Samuel P. Heintzelman, commanding Third corps, noted the wondrous effects that music contributed to a dismal situation:

> Our soldiers, weary and exhausted by the labors of the siege of Yorktown, had left Sunday morning as soon as those in the trenches the night before joined us. The long march through the rain and mud gave but little time for rest. Many straggled or came back with the constant stream of the wounded, who had to be helped to the rear. They were not always prompt to rejoin their regiments.
>
> The rain, the sight of the wounded, the re-enforcements still behind, all conspired to depress everybody. No efforts I could make would move them. I ordered the drums to beat, but the drums were wet, and did not give forth cheerful sounds. I saw some brass instruments. I ordered the musicians to play, but it was only part of a band.
>
> Lieutenant Johnson, of my staff, looked around and found some more. Putting them together, the band struck up a patriotic air. This inspired new life into all. The men collected and began to cheer. The strains were wafted through the old forest, and made themselves heard by our weary troops above the roar of the battle, and inspired them with fresh vigor to perform new deeds of valor. [274]

In October, 1863, Union Col. Samuel W. Price, 21st Kentucky, reported how sounds of music inspired soldiers:

> The command had not proceeded far before firing became heavy on the left of the road, so much so that a company was then deployed as skirmishers in that direction to protect the flank. The men advanced slowly, driving the enemy (cheering all the while, inspired by the soul-stirring music of the band) some twenty-five or thirty minutes. [275]

Music also enhanced listeners' physical strength and endurance. A fast-paced melody or a rousing martial tune could inject instant energy and squeeze another few miles from a marching column of exhausted and foot-weary soldiers.

Although regimental bands were too extravagant for armies to maintain, they were, nevertheless, appreciated by those that witnessed their importance to the morale of troops. Union Lt. Col. George Sangster, commanding a camp of paroled prisoners released after their capture at the battle of Fredericksburg, pleaded to keep the band of the 114th Pennsylvania Volunteers:

> ....My reasons for wishing to retain them are that they have an immense influence through the medium of the national and other airs played upon the disorganized and undisciplined command I am entrusted with, so much so that its effects are very viable to any one acquainted with the camp before and since their arrival. The band is used morning and night, at funerals and all arrivals and departures of men of this camp and has a great tendency to keep the men together and from straggling, saving much trouble and annoyance in the absence of a sufficient guard. [276]

On a more technical level, one soldier's buddy seemed more interested in the musical tone made by bullets than their potential danger . He commented:

> Soon came the singing of the minnies overhead. There is a peculiar tuneful pitch in the flight of these little leaden balls; a musical ear can study the different tones as they skim through the space. A comrade lying next to me, an amateur musician of no mean merit, spoke of this. Said he, "I caught the pitch of the minnie that just passed. It was a swell from E flat to F, and as it retrograded in the distance receded to D—a very pretty change." [277]

Alcohol

"Bottled courage"

Considering the large number of courts-martial relating to drunkenness on duty, it is apparent alcohol played a significant role in relieving stress. Many found intoxication to be a temporary means to reinforce their resolve and supplied a boost in courage necessary to perform tasks. Using alcohol, however, clouded the ability to think and suppressed the perception of danger, perhaps too much. [278]

Officers, more so than the enlisted men, seemed to have been afflicted with the temptation of using spirits. Perhaps they had easier access to it. Federal Col. Charles Wainwright, commanding 1st corps artillery, observed an intoxicated division commander during the retreat through Gettysburg on July 1st:

> ...Brigades and divisions were pretty well mixed up. Still the men were not panic stricken; most of them were talking and joking. As I pushed through the crowd as rapidly as possible, I came across General Rowley, who was in command of the Third Division. He was very talkative, claiming that he was in

command of the corps. I tried to reason with him, showing that Wadsworth and several others ranked him; but soon finding that he was drunk, I rode on to the top of Cemetery Hill. [When Gen. Rowley withdrew towards Gettysburg, he fell off his horse and had to be helped out of a ditch. Later that day he was arrested and removed from the battlefield under guard. His next duty assignment was a draft office in Maine.] [279]

Some needed alcohol reinforcement beyond occasional imbibing. At Chattanooga in 1861, Colonel S. A. M. Wood, 7th Alabama Volunteers, complained to Major-Gen. Bragg:

> Upon my return here I find that Brigadier-General Carroll, of the Provisional Army, formerly postmaster at Memphis, Tenn., is here with two more Tennessee regiments and one company of flying artillery. General Carroll has just been appointed. He has been drunk not less than five years. He is stupid, but easily controlled. He knows nothing, and I believe I can do with him pretty much as I please. [280]

In March, 1863, Union Col. John McNeil, 2nd Missouri State Militia Cavalry, shared an interesting incident:

> The war steed of General Thompson, which proved to be a mare heavy with foal, fell into our hands, and the last that was heard of this doughty hero he was floating down the Saint Francis, the solitary tenant of a dug-out, quite drunk and very melancholy. [281]

Enlisted men were just as tempted to use spirits but were confined in the ranks and subjected to more restricted access than their officers. A sensible officer, with minimal foresight, knew that one of the first things to be done when an army was intermingled with civilian society was to ban liquor sales at local establishments. Lax enforcement of this rule caused a significant loss of manpower when it was needed most. In the Gettysburg campaign, for example, a number of men escaped the battle and reduced the Army of the Potomac's fighting strength at a critical moment. Capt. George Thayer of the 2nd Massachusetts later related:

> Two features of our march through Frederick come to me with vivid impression—the enthusiasm of the people as we passed through their streets with such cheering and displays of the American flag as our men had not witnessed since the days when they marched from home; and the general drunkenness of the army.
> I know nothing of the sobriety of the officers; certainly those of my

acquaintance had too much anxiety to get their men safely out of the town to stop for any hilarity. But abundant whisky, sold on every hand despite the vigilance of the provost-guard, thrust upon the men by well-meaning citizens, put into the midst of our companions as we marched, and drank before we could break the bottles, which we did most promptly and inexorably, threatened a general demoralization of the rank and file, and did leave hundreds of them within my limited observation reeling in the streets, lying in the ruts in perilous proximity to artillery wheels, or snoring by the roadsides far beyond the town. [282]

Major General Slocum, Union 12th corps commander, communicated to General Meade that "When I left Frederick, there were a great number of men from every corps in the army lying about the streets, beastly drunk. I think it important that a cavalry force should be sent back to bring them…" [283]

In June, 1862, Maj. George M. Waddill, 53rd Virginia, described an alcohol-related benefit his unit received in the course of combat:

> As the regiment has not yet come in, a list of its casualties cannot now be made out, but it is believed to be small. When the long-continued and terrible fire to which the regiment was exposed is considered, a small list of casualties would seem to be miraculous, and can only be explained by the facts that our men were deployed as skirmishers, well concealed and protected, and that the enemy were so drunk they could not shoot. This latter view is known to be correct, as prisoners taken were found to be intoxicated. [284]

One lucky man survived his ordeal *because* of his drunken condition. In June, 1864, Union Col. John B. Rogers, 2nd Missouri State Militia Cavalry crossed paths with this fortunate soul:

> Our men came upon 6 guerrillas at Sikeston about sunset last night, and succeeded in killing the notorious guerrilla Wright. The others escaped, but some of them were wounded, and there was blood on the trail. They took 1 prisoner; he was too drunk to kill. [285]

Leave

Allowing soldiers to take leave from their military life was a helpful diversion that promoted coping with dangers on the battlefield. It was a restorative break to repair both the body and mind. This brief respite from the rigors of war provided an unstressed atmosphere for rest and decompression; it permitted men the opportunity to alleviate problems that developed at home during their absence; it recharged them in preparation for returning to a world that drained their strength and spirit.

Animals

One of the few unbroken bonds from civilian life that carried into the military was the affection for animals. Soldiers had their pets, units had their mascots—pleasurable diversions from their harsh existence. Viewed endearingly by their guardians as creatures with human traits, pets and mascots epitomized bravery and loyalty. They inspired the troops and reminded them of their former life. Pets broke the boredom, provided a great outlet for amusement, and gave them the opportunity to express tactile affection.

Armies were accompanied by a large menagerie of interesting subjects. Most were the usual household or farm variety—horses, mules, dogs, and some cats. Their names ranged from the ordinary to the unique. Horses sported lofty or affable monikers such as Methuselah, Charlemagne, Rienzi, Redeye, Little Sorrel, and Kangaroo. Dogs' names had more of a human ring to them such as Sallie, Jack, Old Harvey, York, Major, and Calamity.

Other pets were only slightly unusual such as chickens [Gen. Lee had Henrietta, until someone ate it.]. Others included pigs, donkeys, sheep, badgers, raccoons, and an eagle. The more bizarre animals accompanying the troops included a bear, a wildcat, a camel, and a pelican.

- The 3rd Louisiana CSA, had a donkey. It would push into the commander's tent and try to sleep with him, mistaking the officer for his original owner.
- The 12th Wisconsin Volunteers had a tame bear that accompanied the men all the way to Missouri.
- The mascot of the 43rd Mississippi Infantry was killed by a minie ball during the siege of Vicksburg. It was a camel named Douglas.
- The 9th Connecticut Infantry had a trained pig named "Jeff Davis". Jeff could stand on his hind legs, hold a pipe, and perform many other tricks. He made an amusing sight at inspections.
- An Arkansas unit had a wildcat.
- A Louisiana regiment had a pelican.
- Louis Pfieff, 3rd Illinois Infantry, was accompanied by his dog he brought from home. Pfieff was killed at Shiloh. His faithful dog remained at his master's gravesite for 12 days, only leaving to search for food. [286]

Incident of battle *CEFH/LICW*

It would be unfortunate to ignore the fear endured by the non-human creatures that were an integral part of armies and their campaigns. What kept them from escaping in the midst of danger? Did they fear death? Did they have compassion for the deaths of fellow animals? What reaction did they have to see their master's death?

Official recognition of animals' role in battle is mostly impersonal in nature. Battle reports praise heroic deeds of humans. Animals are usually mentioned only in terms of numbers lost. They are too frequently described as an anonymous presence, un-suffered, and an under-appreciated statistic on a request list for replacement.

Their presence, however, was appreciated and beloved by those who were in direct contact. One Confederate officer paid homage to the sacrifices of the horse:

> …whose starvation and sufferings and wounds and death I really believe used to affect me even more than the like experience of my human fellow-beings; and this because, as [one man said,] "the men '[en]'listed ter git killed, and the horses didn't." Some of these sensitive creatures were mortally afraid of artillery fire. I have seen the poor brutes, when the shells were flying low and close above their backs, squat until their bellies almost touched the ground. [287]

Historians have estimated that 75,000 animals (horses and mules) were present in the Gettysburg campaign. Many horses were at or near the front line ridden by officers, staff, couriers, cavalrymen, or as draught animals. Up to 5,000 animals were killed in the battle.

The number wounded, more than likely, exceeded those killed by several times over. Horses made big targets. Federal Lt. Col. Freeman McGilvery, commanding 1st Volunteer Brigade at Gettysburg, reported what happened to his horse: "During the engagement my horse was hit four times in the fore-shoulder and breast by musketry, once on the fore-leg by shell, and once on the hip by spent solid shot, of which wounds he soon after died." [288]

Draught horses established an almost human bond with their drivers and equine "teammates." One Confederate described it:

> [Draught horses seemed] satisfied during battle, or at least entirely quiet, if their drivers remained with them, especially on their backs; and when the men were compelled to absent themselves for a time and returned again to their teams, I have heard the horses welcome them with whinnies of satisfaction and content, and have seen them, under fire, rub their heads against their drivers with confiding and appealing affection.
>
> And the poor animals loved not only their drivers but each other. I have heard and seen a horse, whose mate was killed at his side, utter an agonized and terrified neigh, meanwhile shuddering violently, and have known a horse so bereaved persistently refuse to eat, and pine away and die. [289]

Other creatures were caught up in the storm of battle. Animals, both wild and domestic, suddenly had their peaceful world swept up and cast into an unknown convulsion of noise and destruction as tens of thousands of humans invaded their world.

During the cannonade at Gettysburg, Union Capt. Samuel Fiske observed the animals' reaction to the storm of gunfire across the landscape: "It was touching to see the little birds, all out of their wits with fright, flying wildly about amidst the tornado of terrible missiles and uttering strange notes of distress. It was touching to see the innocent cows and calves, feeding in the fields, torn in pieces by the shells." [290]

At Gettysburg on July 2nd, skirmishers of the 11th Massachusetts were posted in the fields west of the Emmitsburg Road near the Peter Rogers farm. As the Union line was rolled up from their left, their attention was interrupted from this mortal danger by a seemingly more important problem—a snake rustling through the grass as the men withdrew to their main line.

During this withdrawal the Rogers house was honeycombed with Confederate bullets. Anyone inside must have been stunned by the disturbance. Lt. Henry Blake witnessed one occupant seeking safety: "A kitten, mewing piteously, ran from [the house], jumped upon the shoulders of one of the men and remained there a few minutes during the fight." [291]

Also on July 2nd, near Devil's Den, Henry J. Hunt, Chief of Artillery of the Army of the Potomac, was caught in a melee of cattle stampeded by exploding shells. One unfortunate creature was blown up while wounding some others. The poor animals were confused in finding an escape route to safety. Hunt escaped the terrorized brutes but said he was "badly demoralized" from the experience. [292]

Limits to Diversion Benefits

There were boundaries as to what diversions could do to help soldiers cope with dangerous situations, maintain morale, and hold discipline in the battle line. This was especially true during heavy combat where thick smoke and deafening gunfire precluded movement or prevented hearing any instructive coaxing to divert attention. At that point, coping depended on a soldier's individual fortitude.

The effects of battle eventually cancelled the beneficial effects which natural diversions provided as well as any artificial attempts to maintain focus. Sobering sights of horrific wounds, sounds of men dying, and comrades shot down before one's eyes were all potent distractions away from soldiers' tasks. Such sights triggered emotions which sometimes overrode performing the work at hand and interfered with officers' control of the situation.

Fear as a weapon

You can discover what your enemy fears most by observing the means he uses to frighten you. Eric Hoffer

Commanders saw firsthand what fear could do to their troops when under fire. Consequently, it behooved them to inflict the same fear upon the enemy. It was used as a weapon to degrade an adversary's fighting effectiveness and increase the odds of winning. Confederate General John Gordon, in his *Reminiscences*, noted the "vast difference in accuracy when the enemy was firing back." He used an anecdote to explain:

> A woodsman who was noted as a "crack shot" among his hunting companions felt sure that he was going to win fame as a select rifleman in the army; for he said that in killing a squirrel he always put the bullet through the head, though the squirrel might be perched at the time on the topmost tree limb of the tallest tree. An Irishman who had seen service in the Mexican War, and was attentively listening to this young hunter's boast, fixed his twinkling eye upon the aspiring rifleman and said to him: "Yes; but Dan, me boy, ye must ricollict that the squirrel had no gon in his hand to shoot back at ye." [293]

Gordon further noted that when the enemy fired back it was "one cause of the wild and aimless firing which wasted more tons of lead in battle than all its dead victims would weigh." [294]

Catching the enemy off guard with a surprise attack or flank assault induced fear and used to wreck the enemy's fighting spirit. Stonewall Jackson's shock attack against the Union 11th corps at Chancellorsville, for example, triggered an unstoppable stampede to the rear.

Stampede at Chancellorsville *ACR/B & L*

The most effective weapon for inducing fear on an enemy was artillery fire. Ever since its introduction, cannonades were some of the best means of eroding the enemy's strength, lowering morale, and disuniting enemy troops. They sapped the resolve that kept troops manning the front line, impeded responses to commands, and destroyed confidence in winning. The constant pounding of the line and viewing mounting casualties in the ranks wore away collective spirit and determination. [Today, this operation is known as "shock and awe."]

Since enemy artillery fire was almost always out of range of small arms, little could be done by infantrymen on the receiving end to suppress the source of danger. Even when little or no damage was inflicted, artillery fire could, on occasion, break an attack, even before it began, just from its psychological effects.

The psychological suffering created from cannonades stemmed from the limited options troops had to remedy their situation. A fighting force, pinned down by artillery fire, was deprived of coping with the situation in a direct manner.

Inaction breeds doubt and fear. Action breeds confidence and courage.
Dale Carnegie

The most difficult thing in combat was, according to one veteran, "to be afraid and sit still," while others lying around you bled quietly. Many World War II veterans testified that the harshest, fear-producing experience they endured in combat was their immobilization for hours or days from artillery or mortar fire.

World War II veteran, Lt. Charles Jordan, 9th Division, wrote: "The fear of death came openly when I was lying in a ditch, or a hole, or on the ground and artillery or mortar shells were exploding around me. There was absolutely nothing positive to do about these situations except lay there and pray." [295]

Union 1st Lt. Smith recollected his men's discomfort during the July 3rd cannonade at Gettysburg:

> All this time our nerves were strung to the highest pitch; water ran from every pore in the skin like squeezing a wet sponge, and our clothes were wringing wet. It was nature's provision for our safety, as it prevented total collapse of the nervous system, and the mind from going out in darkness. [296]

Confederates waiting for the end of the artillery duel at Gettysburg July 3rd. ACR/B & L

Artillery fire also destroyed the invincible feeling held by an overconfident enemy readying itself for an attack. Even though Civil War artillery fire caused comparatively small numbers of casualties and the overall physical effects were modest [artillery casualties were less than 10%], it could cause the greatest mental stress. Bullets wounds were bad enough, but when cannon fire was accurate, the visual destruction on men and animals was horrifying. Any soldier on the receiving end of an artillery projectile and who witnessed its shocking effects recognized artillery's deterrent potential.

A Confederate artilleryman at Sailor's Creek, April, 1865 said:

A good many had been wounded and several killed, when a twenty-pounder Parrott shell struck immediately in my front, on the line, nearly severing a man in twain, and hurling him bodily over my head, his arms hanging down and his hands almost slapping me in the face as they passed.

In that one awful moment I distinctly recognized young Blount, who had gazed into my face so intently Sunday night; and but for that peculiar paralysis which in battle sometimes passes upon a man's entire being— excepting only his fighting powers—the recognition might have been too much for me.

In a few moments the artillery fire ceased and I had time to glance about me and note results a little more carefully. I had seldom seen a fire more accurate, nor one that had been more deadly, in a single regiment, in so brief a time. The expression of the men's faces indicated clearly enough its effect upon them. They did not appear to be hopelessly demoralized, but they did look blanched and haggard and awe-struck. [297]

At Fort Harrison near Richmond, Federal Brig. Gen. Edward H. Ripley was standing directly behind an artilleryman when he was suddenly "dashed in the face with a hot steaming mass of something horrible" that covered his eyes and filled his nose and mouth. "I thought my head had gone certainly this time," Ripley continued:

A staff officer happened to have a towel with which he cleaned away the disgusting mass from my face and opened my eyes; unbuttoning my sabre belt and throwing open my blouse, I threw out a mass of brains, skull, hair and blood. As I opened my eyes the headless trunk of the artilleryman lay between my feet with the blood gurgling out. [298]

The eroding effects on the enemy's spirit was important enough to be included in the instructions for each artillery piece's "Table of Fire," a chart pasted under the lids of ammunition chests. The chart was used to set barrel elevations, determine the ranges of projectiles, and time settings for explosive rounds. The table instructed that the use of shell was "to produce a moral rather than a physical effect."

Denial, Acclimation, Acceptance

One of the things which danger does to you after a time is -, well, to kill emotion. I don't think I shall ever feel anything again except fear. None of us can hate anymore - or love. Graham Greene - The Confidential Agent (1939)

The final stages of coping with the dangers of combat were denial, acclimation, and acceptance. Adaptation was the only way of surviving an environment which would otherwise lead to insanity.

For some, denial was used as a means to maintain some mental sense of normalcy. It was a "this is not happening to me" feeling. As mentioned earlier, pinned down soldiers were left with few choices. A physical solution not being practical, left the men to confront the situation with a mental response. Coping, in this case, may have been simply to block out the fact that the threat even existed or, at least, to mentally escape the danger through denial.

One consequence of this stress was tunnel vision . According to James Lucas, an infantryman from World War II, denial contributed to visually blocking out danger: "No infantryman sees at any one time during an attack anymore than 200 meters ahead of him or much on either side of him. It is easy...to concentrate upon one particular item to the exclusion of all others. On the battlefield this blinkered view is [partially due] to men's desire not to look too closely at dangers they can do little about." [299]

Denial was also a way to soften the unexpected blow of a defeat. At Gettysburg, John Collins, 8th Pa. Cavalry, relayed his experience as a prisoner accompanying the Confederate retreat while being guarded by remnants of Pickett's division:

> I told [a Confederate] officer [of Pickett's division] as politely as I could that I thought they were badly beaten, and would hardly get across the Potomac. He laughed and said that they were not trying to get across,—that Baltimore was their objective point just then; from there, he explained, it was but a forced march to Washington, and once there they could conquer a peace in thirty days. His hopes amused me; I remembered that when retreating from the Chickahominy and from Chancellorsville I did not know anything of defeat, but thought I was marching to victory by another road. [300]

The supreme change necessary for combat veterans, if they were to continue performing their duties as soldiers, was to somehow adjust and view horrors as a normal circumstance. Men, steeped in death, surrounded by groans of the wounded and screams of the dying, acclimated themselves into hardened soldiers succumbing to an existence, devalued of humanity, where the termination of life, massive destruction, and perpetual suffering must be accepted as commonplace.

One observer noted that "the dread and sickening loathing created by many a corpse on a battlefield is by familiarity and constant view transformed into a stoical indifference. Were this not so, the awful carnage of some battles would have made deserters of thousands of soldiers." [301]

Veterans soberly adapted to the depredations and realities of warfare. At Goose Creek, June 21st, 1863. Federal Captain Robert Carter, 1st U. S. Artillery (Heavy) reminisced:

> Dead and dying horses were thickly strewn about on the banks of the stream, and in the marsh. As we plodded along the turn-pike, some 'bummer' discovered an amputated arm, with hand and outstretched fingers, lying in the road and partially covered with dust, near a house where some surgeons had thoughtlessly thrown it. The temptation proved too much; he gave it a slight kick with his toe, probably to see what it was, but that was enough. It became a foot-ball for everyone, and had to run the gauntlet from the head of the brigade to the rear, along the road to Upperville. [302]

A Confederate veteran noted another occasion at Spottsylvania,:

> During the long and fierce struggle I saw soldiers place the arms of their comrades who had just fallen in such a position as when they had become stiffened they would hold the cartridges we were using. Yes, fighting and exhausted, amidst blood and mud and brains, they would sit on the bodies of their fallen comrades for rest, and dared not show even a finger above the breastworks, for so terrible was the fire at this angle that a tree eighteen inches in diameter was cut asunder by minnie balls. [303]

Another Confederate officer noted:

> The six brigades of General Magruder's command—Barksdale's, to which we were attached, being one—had arrived at Frazier's farm the preceding night after dark and too late to take part in the engagement. We were overpowered with fatigue, intent only on sleep, and sank to rest amid the wreck and death of the hard-fought field.
>
> In the shadowy dawn, as our guns, moving into position to reopen the fight, threaded their way through the confused bivouac of the slumbering, the dying and the dead—the mysterious hush of the battle-field resting over all—we saw, side by side, upturned together to the bleaching dew, the pale faces of the breathing and the breathless

sleepers, not distinguishable in the dim morning twilight.

Suddenly the drums beat to arms and the living rose,—and then the stolidest veteran in that vast multitude shuddered as he left the side of his ghastly bedfellow who had rested with him so quietly all that summer night, and by whose side the frame that now shrank away with horror might rest to-night as ghastly as he. [304]

That same officer described the march toward the Chickahominy in 1862:

A ghastly scene was spread across the road hard by. The Seventeenth and Twenty-first Mississippi, of our brigade, had been ordered into the woods about dusk the evening before and told not to fire into the first line they met; but the poor fellows ran into a Federal brigade and were shocked and staggered by a deadly volley. Splendid soldiers that they were, they obeyed orders, held their own fire, laid down and took the enemy's. Almost every man struck was killed, and every man killed shot through the brain.

Their comrades had gone into the woods as soon as it was light, brought out the bodies and laid them in rows, with hands crossed upon the breast, but eyes wide-staring. A sickly summer rain had fallen in the night and the faces of the dead were bleached with more than death's pallor. Every eyeball was strained upward toward the spot where the bullet had crashed through the skull, and every forehead stained with ooze and trickle of blood. Men were passing through the silent lilies, bending low, seeking in the distorted faces to identify their friends. [305]

And still another occasion:

[At Martinsburg, W. Va.] While thus marching and countermarching amidst a murderous fire, a canon-ball struck in the colorguard, just in the rear of my horse's tail, cut one man asunder, tore off the skull of another, which was thrown in front, and spattered blood and brains on all who were near. My veterans, instead of being stampeded, only pressed a little more impulsively upon my horse's tail. [306]

Beyond the initial shock of combat, acclimation and, finally, acceptance offered the last means of mental escape. One Confederate Civil War veteran described his acclimatized view of battle:

We [were] coming to the period…when we might fairly claim to have been soldiers indeed; when the disjointed fragments had at last been welded into an army. We had been "shooted over" and even "blooded"; had heard the screech of the shell and the hiss of minie balls, and had learned to discount their deadliness in some measure….

Soldiers are but human, and the veterans who have been in battle before know what is implied in the work ahead and that some—and it may be one as well as another—will probably not answer at the next roll-call. The "eagerness for the fray" of which we read so often, rarely survives the first battle; in all that follows, it is conspicuously absent, however the men may have gained in steadiness and have acquired self-possession under fire. [307]

Confederate veteran, George Cary Eggleston, described the evolution of soldiers from impetuous enlistees, to disciplined warriors, to men freely, almost anxiously, accepting the inevitability of their mortal ending:

> The men who early in the war struggled for a place in the front rank, whenever there was chance of a fight, and thought themselves unlucky if they failed to get it, are the men who gave character afterwards to the well-organized and well-disciplined army which so long contested the ground before Richmond.
> They did become soldiers after a while, well regulated and thoroughly effective. The process of disciplining them took away none of their personal spirit or their personal interest in the war, but it taught them the value of unquestioning obedience, and the virtue there was in yielding it....
> I think hardly any man in that army entertained a thought of coming out of the struggle alive. The only question with each was when his time was to come, and a sort of gloomy fatalism took possession of many minds. Believing that they must be killed sooner or later, and that the hour and the manner of their deaths were unalterably fixed, many became singularly reckless, and exposed themselves with the utmost carelessness to all sorts of unnecessary dangers.
> "I'm going to be killed pretty soon," said as brave a man as I ever knew, to me one evening. "I never flinched from a bullet until today, and now I dodge every time one whistles within twenty feet of me." I tried to persuade him out of the belief, and even got for him a dose of valerian with which to quiet his nerves. He took the medicine, but assured me that he was not nervous in the least.
> "My time is coming, that's all," he said, "and I don't care. A few days more or less don't signify much." An hour later the poor fellow's head was blown from his shoulders as he stood by my side. [308]

The transformation of civilians to soldiers, to seasoned, battle-hardened veterans shaped an enduring influence on the lives of those that survived. Some of their undying memories were cherished for the unbreakable bonds that were created from the experience. Some memories were full of demons which every veteran fought to overcome. It is hoped that each eventually found inner peace for their sacrifice.

Last Word

Fear, in clinical terms, is merely an awareness to danger. The response to fear, the ability to overcome the involuntary mental and physical reactions to fear, and to manage fear are the mystical uncertainties which each soldier faces. The capacity to override the potent inner forces of self-preservation in exchange for the willingness to relinquish everyone's most valued possession—life, calls for the rest of society to venerate those that volunteer themselves to participate and suffer such great sacrifices.

It is difficult to comprehend how Civil War soldiers or, for that matter, the men and women of any war, endured the brutal life they experienced. Machiavelli once said, "Who ought to be fonder of peace than soldiers whose life is placed in jeopardy by war?" [309]

Those that survive war contemplate their ordeal in private, talk with those who shared the common experience, but they could never convey the hellish events to those that didn't. Robert H. Scales, Maj. Gen., U. S. Army, retired, wrote of the brotherhood created on the battlefield:

> Someday, we will all join those who are serving so gallantly now and have preceded us on the battlefield from Gettysburg to Wanat…We will join with a band of brothers to recount the experience of serving something greater than ourselves.
>
> I believe in my very soul that the Almighty reserves a corner of heaven, probably around a perpetual campfire, where someday we can meet and embrace all of the band of brothers throughout the ages, to tell our stories while envious bystanders watch and wonder how horrific and incendiary the crucible of violence must have been to bring such a disparate assemblage so close to the hand of God. [310]

To all who served, this book is dedicated.

Epilogue

Since the Civil War, science has made significant advances in studying and treating injuries of the mind. Military experiments are underway to try to predict who are high risks for post-traumatic stress disorder. One test flashes a series of contrasting images across a screen to a participant wired with electrodes. A dog sniffing a bloody corpse followed by an attractive movie star in a sexy top, for example, creates a response in the candidate and registers the number of blinks to perhaps determine patterns and effects.

Such experiments may lead to determining the triggers of PTSD and help reduce the burden of returning veterans suffering from the mental wounds of combat. Today, veterans returning from a war zone are given a post-deployment survey to better assess the effects of their experience. The feedback form asks troops such questions as "Did you ever see a corpse?", "Were you exposed to noxious smoke or gas, etc.?", "Did you fire your weapon at the enemy?".

The prospects for solutions to repairing wounds of the mind are challenging. Military doctors have yet to figure why some veterans exposed to the same experience are traumatized while others are not. Some believe, justifiably, there is a direct correlation between the prevalence of PTSD and the number of deployments to war zones. [311]

Today, military techniques employ methods to deter the negative effects individuals face in combat. Is it possible for the military to teach or condition a person to be less anxious and less fearful so that he can function under stress? Today's American army thinks so. Whereas Civil War training hoped to control men on the battlefield by instilling discipline through intense drill practice, and maintaining morale by employing various techniques, it did not address how to deal with fear. That was left up to each soldier.

Today's military openly confronts the subject of fear in a concept known as *Battlemind*. The program is comprehensive, instructive, and tackles a subject

161

more thoroughly than previous preparedness training that was either never included or only lightly covered. It addresses mental stress and coping and is designed to fortify soldiers' "inner strength to face adversity, fear, and hardship during combat with confidence and resolution." It provides "tough facts" about combat and offers what soldiers may see, hear, smell, think, and feel during the chaos of battle and "what warriors should know and do in preparing for war."

The legacy of *Battlemind*, however, is yet to be written. [For a detailed description of the program, refer to the appendices that follow.]

Appendix A

Today's Preparedness Training for Soldiers

[Note that the U.S. Army has adopted a policy of capitalizing the "s" in soldier and "w" in warrior. The Marines have capitalized Marine for years and the Army merely followed suit. However, in most writing by non-Army members soldier is still small case.]

Battlemind is "a Soldier's inner strength to face adversity, fear, and hardship during combat with confidence and resolution. It is the will to persevere and win." Its objective is "to develop those factors (focusing on Leader behaviors) that contribute to the Soldier's will and spirit to fight and win in combat, thereby reducing combat stress reactions." The program instructs that:

- Combat is sudden, intense, and life threatening.
- It is the job of the Soldier to kill the enemy.
- No soldier in combat knows how he will perform until the moment arrives.

Preparing today's soldiers for combat entails in-depth training, including discussions on a detailed list of emotional and physical expectations and reactions to battle. It teaches:

Tough Facts About Combat

Fear in combat is common.

Reality and Actions: Findings: • Even heroes feel fear. Over two-thirds of silver star recipients reported an increase in fear as the battle progressed. • Common symptoms of fear include: violent shaking or trembling, losing control of bowels or bladder, feeling weak, having cold sweats, and vomiting. •Fear and anxiety are reduced in combat when Warriors engage in actions derived from their training experiences.

What Leaders Can Do: • Drill and train Warriors in specific actions to take under combat conditions. • Provide Warriors sufficient time to recover physically and mentally from combat. • Admitting and joking about fear will release tension. • Remember that fear is a normal response and NOT a mental disorder. • All Warriors are entitled to go into combat with the best chance of survival that you as their Leader can provide.

There will be communication and information breakdown.

Reality and Actions: Findings: • Warriors report that deployment policies are often inconsistently applied. • Warriors often report that they don't know the status of their wounded team members. • Warriors make up rumors if Leaders don't tell them the facts.

What Leaders Can Do: • Keep your Warriors informed. Telling your Warriors you don't know is better than not telling them anything at all. Make sure that your policies and views on all matters are clearly expressed and made known. Let every Warrior in the unit know the status of wounded evacuees.• Disseminate the news of your successes, as well as those of other units. Effective communication is the responsibility of the Leader.

Warriors frequently perceive failures in Leadership.

Reality and Actions: Findings: • Good Leadership is linked to high Warrior morale and cohesion and to fewer mental health problems. • Warriors report that frequently Leaders engage in actions to enhance their own career and personal well-being. • Warriors also report that Leaders often fail to exhibit clear thinking and reasonable action when under stress.

What Leaders Can Do: • Have experienced Leaders tell unit members facts they wish they had known in order to mentally prepare for combat. • Allow subordinates to seek clarification of orders or policies without being defensive or considering them disloyal. • Remove or reassign those subordinate Leaders or Warriors who fail to measure up. • Recognize how stress and lack of sleep affect your decisions.

Courage and valor in combat are the measures of Warrior and Leader performance.

Combat impacts every Warrior mentally and emotionally.

Reality and Actions: Findings: • Combat operational stress reactions involve many symptoms (physical, mental, behavioral) and occur when a Warrior becomes overwhelmed with the stressors of combat. • Over 95% of Warriors who receive forward mental health support are returned to duty. Combat operational stress reactions are expected. • Reactions that are sometimes called PTSD can help Warriors survive in combat. For example, being hyper-alert or startling easily. • Most Warriors (80-90%) do not develop PTSD but some need help. • "Mild traumatic brain injury" (MTBI) is a medical term for concussion (being knocked out, getting your bell rung). Full recovery is expected after concussion but prompt medical evaluation is necessary to assure there is not a more severe brain injury.

The combat environment is harsh and demanding.

Reality and Actions: Findings: • A Warriors' mental performance progressively deteriorates with less than 8 hours of sleep per day. 5 to 6 hours of sleep per 24 hours is not sufficient. • The combat environment (e.g., physical strain, heat, noise, lack of privacy) takes a toll on all Warriors. • Warriors are extremely sensitive to perceived inequalities in MWR resource distribution. [The acronym MWR [Morale, Welfare, and Recreation] is commonly used on military bases to refer to services for soldiers such as internet cafes, sports complexes, movie theatres etc.]

What Leaders Can Do: • Ensure unit members replenish lost sleep. Make sleep a priority like other essential logistical re-supply items. • Insist on a fair distribution of MWR resources. Prevent double standards among Officers, NCOs and Junior Enlisted Warriors. • Be aware of the physical condition and sleep patterns of your Warriors and insist that conditioning and sleep are maintained throughout the deployment.

Combat poses moral and ethical challenges.

Reality and Actions: My unit leadership might treat me differently. I would be seen as weak. My leaders would blame me for the problem. Members of my unit might have less confidence in me. It would harm my career. Findings: Only 25-40% of Warriors with behavioral health problems seek help because they report numerous stigmatizing beliefs regarding their unit members and Leadership. • Combat exposes the reality of death. • Combat tests the character of Leaders and Warriors alike. • Warriors who are unable to control their anger are more likely to commit ethical violations.

The American Warrior: "The capacity of Soldiers for absorbing punishment and enduring privations is almost inexhaustible so long as they believe they are getting a square deal, that their commanders are looking out for them, and that their own accomplishments are understood and appreciated." Gen. Dwight Eisenhower, 1944 [312]

Appendix B

Pre-Deployment Battlemind For Leaders

Objectives of Battlemind:

To prepare Warriors mentally for the rigors of combat and other military deployments

To prepare Warriors with the skills to assist their battle-buddy during deployment as well as to transition back home

The Chaos of Combat Includes:

Intense elation, fatigue and fear.
Heat, noise, blast effects
Tough to discriminate targets
Difficulty identifying Leaders
Hard to maintain contact, control of movement
Disorder from many yelling commands simultaneously; injured screaming
Concentration on wounded and/or dead
Elusive enemy; rarely visible, poorly defined
"Worst Day" Scenarios
      Your battle-buddy is killed or critically wounded
      Key Leader killed
      Missing Warriors
      Catastrophic vehicle kill or accident
      Perimeter breach
      Handling/cleaning-up of human remains

What You May See

Extreme poverty
Decay, garbage and feces
People on rooftops; gawkers "just looking"
Rubbled structures
Incoming/outgoing fire
Raging infernos –your vehicle on fire
Wounded/killed friends and enemies

What You May Hear

Explosions
Gunfire, ricochets and near misses
Cries of wounded
Pleas for help or mercy
Wailing of mourners
Shouts of rage and taunts
Multiple commands

What You May Smell

Rotting garbage
Burnt flesh and hair
Heavy chemical and industrial smoke/fuel
Open sewage, feces and stale urine
Decaying animals

What You May Think

There'll always be war here; always has been
I'm wasting my life here
They should be fighting for themselves
They don't want us here
There doesn't seem to be a point to this
The sacrifices I'm making are not worth it
No progress is being made here
I'm tired of this s***!

What You May Feel

Emotional:
Anger, fear, doubt, isolation, worry
Confusion
Second guessing; feelings of guilt
Pride, excitement
Camaraderie, cohesion
Physical:
Pain, nausea
Muscle soreness; periods of profound exhaustion
Other physical effects

The Nature of Operational Deployments

The realities:
Boredom and monotony
A lack of privacy
Perceptions of a lack of necessary equipment
Rules of Engagement / General Order 1
Orders from the Chain of Command
You are not home

Deployments can strengthen your Battlemind:

Provide an opportunity to lead in combat
Show your courage
Appreciate what's really important in life
Mature as a person and a Warrior
Use your military skills and training
Be part of a dynamic team
Provide an opportunity to serve your country

Mental Toughness: "Leaders must have strong minds, ready to accept facts as they are." Harry S. Truman

Will you have to face these combat facts? How will you react? What can you do to remain mentally tough and confident? What will you do to keep your Warriors resilient?

Appendix C

Pre-Deployment Battlemind For Warriors(Preparing for War: What Warriors Should Know and Do)

"Steel" your Battlemind
Be a battle-buddy
Listen to your Leaders (NCOs and Officers)
Trust your skills and training
Maintain contact back home

What Warriors Should Know: • Fear in combat is common. • Events in combat can appear random and unavoidable. • You will make decisions that impact the lives of others. Trust your skills and training.

Warrior Actions: • Your combat training is world class; trust it. • When under strain, stress or enemy attack, do as you were trained to do. • Admitting and joking about fear may help release tension. • Actively participate and learn from after action reviews.

"You will see events in combat that will test your courage and extend your faith. If you will accept the challenge of always doing what is right and just, these moments of discouragement and setbacks will fall behind you." "You must never quit." Accept the challenge. [313]

Endnotes

1. Paul M. Johnson, *Every Man Has His Breaking Point: The Attitudes of American Infantrymen Towards Combat Fatigue in World War II* [Department of History, University of Wisconsin – Eau Claire, Research Seminar, Professor Thomas Miller, Cooperating Professor: Earl Shoemaker, By Paul M. Johnson, November 28, 2006]
2. Robert H. Scales, Maj. Gen., ret., *"Peaches and Pound Cake"* [*The American Legion Magazine*, January 2010], 40
3. http://www.heartquotes.net/fear.html [All subsequent standalone passages in italics, unless otherwise footnoted, can be accessed from this webpage.]
4. Earl J. Hess, *The Union Soldier in Battle* [Lawrence, University Press of Kansas, 1997], 92
5. Maj. Gen., ret., Robert H. Scales, Jr., "A Battlefield Too Even" [*American Legion Magazine*, 12/2006 issue], 18
6. *OR*, Vol. 30, Part 2, 728
7. Major Gregory A. Daddis, U.S. Army, "Understanding Fear's Effect on Unit Effectiveness," [*Military Review*, July -August 2004], 23
8. Lt. Col. W. T. Poague, "At Gettysburg," *Photographic History f the Civil War: Forts and Artillery*, Vol. 3, [Secaucus, The Blue and Grey Press, 1987], 74
9. Allen C. Redwood, "The Confederate in the Field," *Photographic History of the Civil War—Soldiers Life and Secret Service*, Vol. 4 [Secaucus, The Blue and Grey Press, 1987], 158, 160, 162
10. *Understanding Fear's Effect on Unit Effectiveness,* 23
11. *The Gift of Fear*, Gavin DeBecker [New York, Little, Brown and Company], 1997], 97-100
12. *Understanding Fear's Effect on Unit Effectiveness,* 26; *Citizen Soldier*, Stephan E. Ambrose [New York, Simon and Schuster, 1998], 485
13. *Understanding Fear's Effect on Unit Effectiveness,* 23
14. *Peaches and Pound Cake,* 38
15. *The War of the Rebellion: A Compilation of the Official Records of the Union and Confederate Armies*, 70 vols. In 128 parts, Hereinafter referred to as "*OR*, Vol.__, Part__, __." Unless noted, all references are from Series 1 [U.S. War Department], Vol. 27, Part 1, 1034

16. Scott L. Mingus, Sr., *Human Interest Stories of the Gettysburg Campaign* [Orrtanna, Colecraft Industries, 2006], 70
17. *The Bachelder Papers—Gettysburg in Their Own Words*, 3 Vols: Vols. 1 & 2, 1994, Vol. 3, 1995, Hereinafter referred to as *BP* [Dayton: Morningside House, Inc.], Vol. 1, 215
18. *OR*, Vol. 27, Part 1, 826
19. *OR*, Vol. 27, Part 2, 614
20. *BP*, Vol. 2, 1096
21. *BP*, Vol. 1, 328-30
22. Joshua Chamberlain, *The Passing of the Armies* [Gettysburg, Stan Clark Military Books, 1994], 98-9
23. Paddy Griffith, *Battle Tactics of the Civil War* [New Haven, Yale University Press, 1989], 64
24. *OR*, Vol. 19, Part 1, 1024-25
25. *OR*, Vol. 25, Part 2, 197
26. Richard Holmes, *Acts of War* [New York, The Free Press, 1986], 205
27. Stouffer, Samuel A., et al. *The American Soldier: Combat and its Aftermath. Studies in Social Psychology in World War II,* Vol. 2 [Princeton, Princeton University Press, 1949], 201
28. *Understanding Fear's Effect on Unit Effectiveness,* 24
29. Robert Stiles, Major of Artillery in the Army of Northern Virginia, *Four Years Under Marse Robert* [New York and Washington, The Neale Publishing Company, 1904, third edition], 291 [The electronic version of this work was provided through courtesy of the University of North Carolina at Chapel Hill.]
30. *Every Man Has His Breaking Point: The Attitudes of American Infantrymen Towards Combat Fatigue in World War II*
31. *Understanding Fear's Effect on Unit Effectiveness,* 24
32. *Four Years Under Marse Robert,* 259
33. *OR*, Vol. 10, Part 1, 324
34. *Gettysburg: A Meditation on War and Values,* 239
35. *Understanding Fear's Effect on Unit Effectiveness,* 22
36. Joseph J. Ondishko, Jr., "A View of Anxiety, Fear, and Panic" [*Military Affairs*, Vol. 36, No. 2, Society for Military History, Apr., 1972], 58
37. *Every Man Has His Breaking Point: The Attitudes of American Infantrymen Towards Combat Fatigue in World War II*
38. *Citizen Soldier,* 484-5
39. *War as I knew it*, George S. Patton, Jr. [New York, Bantam Books, 1980], 322
40. Kent Gramm, *Gettysburg: A Meditation on War and Values* [Indianapolis, Indiana University Press, 1994], 239
41. *Understanding Fear's Effect on Unit Effectiveness,* 24
42. Gerald F. Linderman, *Embattled Courage* [New York, The Free Press, 1989], 7

43. David H. Marlowe, *Psychological and Psychosocial Consequences of Combat and Deployment with Special Emphasis on the Gulf War*, Chapter 3 [Rand Corporation, 2000]

44. William F. Fox, Lt. Col., U.S.V., *Fox's Regimental Losses* [Albany Publishing Company, Albany, 1889], Chapter VII, 59

45. *Every Man Has His Breaking Point: The Attitudes of American Infantrymen Towards Combat Fatigue in World War II*

46. Scott Mingus, Sr., *Human Interest Stories of the Gettysburg Campaign,* Vol. 2, [Orrtanna, Colecraft Industries, 2007], 41

47. http://www.civilwarhome.com/desertion2.htm

48. http://en.wikipedia.org/wiki/Adrenaline#Actions_in_the_body

49. Dr. David Harrison, *Adrenaline and Self Defense-Friend or Foe*

50. *Adrenaline and Self Defense-Friend or Foe*; *Understanding Fear's Effect on Unit Effectiveness,*

51. Harry W. Pfanz, *Gettysburg, The Second Day* [Chapel Hill, The University of North Carolina Press, 1987], 224

52. http://en.wikipedia.org/wiki/Adrenaline#Actions_in_the_body; Dr. Ranit Mishori, "Can Stress Make You Sick?" [*Parade Magazine*, 10/25/09]

53. *The American Soldier, Combat and its Aftermath*, Vol. 2, 77

54. *Four Years Under Marse Robert* , 290

55. http://www.clausewitz.com/CWZHOME/On_War/BK1ch07.html

56. *OR*, Vol. 38, Part 2, 534-35

57. *Fox's Regimental Losses,* Chapter VII, 62

58. William Watson, *Life in the Confederate Army* [New York, Scribner and Welford, 1983], 203-04

59. *OR*, Vol.27, Part 1, 348

60. John J. Pullen, *The Twentieth Maine* [Dayton, Morningside Books, 1980], 24

61. *OR*, Vol. 27, Part 3, 467-8

62. Letter of November 21, 1877 from Maj. Scheibert, of The Prussian Royal Engineers, *SHSP*, Vol. 5, 90-91

63. *Human Interest Stories of the Gettysburg Campaign*, 19

64. *Four Years Under Marse Robert* , 327-28

65. *OR*, Vol. 27, Part 2, 677

66. *OR*, Vol. 27, Part 3, 231 NOTE ON ORIGINAL.--Total horses, 207; total mules, 52.

67. *OR*, Vol. 27, Part 3, 842

68. *OR*, Vol. 27, Part 2, 696

69. Stephen Z. Starr, *The Union Cavalry in the Civil War,* Vol. 1[Baton Rouge, Louisiana State University, 1979], 429-30

70. *Acts of War*, 124

71. *Four Years Under Marse Robert*, 348

72. *Fighting for the Confederacy*, 208

73. *War as I Knew it*, 335

74. *Acts of War*, 124
75. *OR*, Vol. 27, Part 1, 862
76. *Acts of War*, 115
77. Col. Thomas Rafferty, U.S.V., Bandy Freeland, and Bearss,eds., *The Gettysburg Papers- Addresses on the War 1861-65*, Vol. 2[Dayton, Morningside Bookshop, 1978], 543
78. *Photographic History of the Civil War-Soldiers Life and Secret Service*, 174
79. *The Life and Letters of George Gordon Meade, Vol. 2*, 110-11
80. *Battle Tactics of the Civil War*, 150-51; Archer Jones, *Civil War Command and Strategy* [New York, The Free Press, 1992], 29-30
81. *OR*, Vol. 27, Part 2, 550
82. *OR*, Vol. 27, Part 3, 378
83. *OR*, Vol. 27, Part 3, 601
84. *Human Interest Stories of the Gettysburg Campaign*, 62
85. *Civil War Artillery at Gettysburg*, 2nd ed., 263
86. *Four Years Under Marse Robert*, 349
87. http://www.clausewitz.com/CWZHOME/On_War/BK1ch06.html
88. *Peaches and Pound Cake*, 38
89. http://en.wikipedia.org/wiki/Health_effects_from_noise
90. *OR*, Vol. 38, Part 2, 151
91. L. A. Smith, 1st Lt., 136th N. Y. Infantry, *The Gettysburg Papers*. 2 Vols. [Morningside Bookshop, 1978], Vol. 1, 345-6
92. Alexander Hunter, "A High Private's Sketch of Sharpsburg." *Southern Historical Society Papers* hereinafter known as *SHSP*, Vol. 11, 15
93. *OR*, Vol. 21, 503
94. Brig. Gen. John Gibbon, *Personal Recollections of the Civil War* [Dayton, Morningside Bookshop, 1988], 161
95. *The Gettysburg Papers*, Vol. 1, 348
96. *The Union Soldier in Battle*, 180
97. *OR*, Vol. 36, Part 1, 264-65
98. Russell F. Weigley, *A Great Civil War* [Indianapolis, Indiana University Press, 2000], 134; *Fox's Regimental Losses*, Chapter VII, 59
99. *Fox's Regimental Losses*, Chapter VII, 59
100. *OR*, Vol. 27, Part 1, 285
101. *OR*, Vol. 27, Part 1, 688
102. *The Gettysburg Papers*, Vol. 1, 346
103. *BP*, Vol. 3, 1363-4
104. *Fox's Regimental Losses*, Chapter VII, 59-60
105. *Four Years Under Marse Robert*, 196-97
106. *Battle Tactics of the Civil War*, 144
107. *OR*, Vol. 27, Part 2, 553
108. *BP*, Vol. 1, 272
109. *The Gettysburg Papers*, Vol. 1, 349

110. *Four Years Under Marse Robert*, 219-220
111. *Four Years Under Marse Robert*, 282
112. *The American Soldier: Combat and its Aftermath. Studies in Social Psychology in World War II,* Vol. 2, 77
113. *Four Years Under Marse Robert*, 349-50
114. Edward Hagerman, *The American Civil War and the Origins of Modern Warfare* [Indianapolis, Indiana University Press, 1988], 207, 265
115. Gary G. Lash, "141st Pa. At Gettysburg" [*Gettysburg Magazine #14*], 98
116. *Four Years Under Marse Robert*, 333
117. John Talbott, "Combat Trauma in the American Civil War" [*History Today*, Vol. 46, March, 1996]
118. *Psychological and Psychosocial Consequences of Combat and Deployment with Special Emphasis on the Gulf War*, Chapter 3
119. *Psychological and Psychosocial Consequences of Combat and Deployment with Special Emphasis on the Gulf War*, Chapter 3
120. *Acts of War*, 255-56; *The American Soldier: Combat and its Aftermath. Studies in Social Psychology in World War II,* Vol. 2, 83
121. *BP*, Vol. 3, 1,360–1,361.
122. *OR*, Vol. 46, Part 1, 259
123. http://www.medterms.com/script/main/art.asp?articlekey=5474
124. *Peaches and Pound Cake*, 39
125. *Embattled Courage*, 268
126. *Embattled Courage,* 268
127. *Citizen Soldier*, Stephan E. Ambrose [Simon and Schuster, New York], 1998, 473
128. *Four Years Under Marse Robert* , 217
129. http://en.wikipedia.org/wiki/Coping_(psychology)
130. *Understanding Fear's Effect on Unit Effectiveness,* 24
131. Paul Fussell, *WARTIME -Understanding and Behavior in the Second World War* [New York, Oxford University Press, 1989], 274
132. *A View of Anxiety, Fear, and Panic*, 58
133. *Fighting for the Confederacy*, 277
134. Richard A. Sauers, *"Rarely Has More Skill, Vigor, or Wisdom Been Shown": George G. Meade on July 3 at Gettysburg*, essay in *Three days at Gettysburg*, Gary Gallagher, ed. [Kent, Kent State University Press, 1999], 234
135. *OR*, Vol. 18, 233
136. Sun Tzu, James Clavell ed., *The Art of War* [Delacorte Press, New York, 1983], 61-62
137. *Fox's Regimental Losses*, Chapter VII, 62-63
138. J. Wm. Jones, [reply to Mr. Cazenove G. Lee, of Washington, in the table, which was published originally in the *Baltimore Sun*.] [From the *Times-Dispatch*, January 8, 1905.], *SHSP*, Vol. 32, 46-47

139. *Citizen Soldier*, Stephan E. Ambrose [Simon and Schuster, New York], 1998, 473
140. *Acts of War*, 24
141. *Peaches and Pound Cake*, 40
142. Rocky Bleier, "A Prayer Remembered" [*The American Legion Magazine*, January 2010], 30
143. *OR* Vol. 31, Part 2, 254
144. *Four Years Under Marse Robert*, 197
145. *OR*, Vol. 27, Part 1, 511
146. *OR*, Vol. 27, Part 1, 868
147. *OR*, Vol. 15, 575
148. *Webster's New Collegiate Dictionary* [Springfield, G. & C. Merriam Company, 1973], 748
149. William Swinton, *Campaigns of the Army of the Potomac* [Secaucus, The Blue and Grey Press, 1988], 256
150. *OR*, Series 2, Vol. 2, 1217
151. Walter Reed Army Institute of Research, U.S. Army Medical Research and Materiel Command, 35
152. *OR*, Vol. 12, Part 3, 148
153. *OR*, Vol. 27, Part 3, 1038-39
154. *OR*, Vol. 27, Part 3, 778-79
155. *War as I Knew it*, 336
156. Herb S. Crum, ed., *The Eleventh Corps Artillery at Gettysburg: The Papers of Major Thomas Ward Osborn, Chief of Artillery* [Hamilton, Edmonston Publishing, Inc., 1991], 44
157. *OR*, Vol. 39, Part 1, 810
158. *OR*, Vol. 12, Part 2, 437
159. *OR*, Vol. 19, Part 1, 217
160. *OR*, Vol. 19, Part 1, 66
161. *OR*, Vol. 27, Part 1, 246-47
162. *Campaigns of the Army of the Potomac*, 255
163. *OR*, Vol. 2, 312
164. *Pickett's Charge*, 234
165. James McPherson, *For Cause and Comrades* [New York, Oxford University Press, 1997], 6
166. *Psychological and Psychosocial Consequences of Combat and Deployment with Special Emphasis on the Gulf War*, Chapter 3
167. *OR*, Vol. 51, Part 2, 1065-66
168. *Four Years Under Marse Robert*, 347
169. *Four Years Under Marse Robert*, 116-17
170. *The Union Soldier in Battle*, 119
171. *OR*, Vol. 36, Part 1, 438
172. *OR*, Vol. 42, Part 1, 865
173. *OR*, Vol. 17, Part 1, 356

174. *OR*, Vol. 17, Part 1, 259
175. *Four Years Under Marse Robert*, 105
176. *Battles and Leaders of the Civil War*, 265, Harry W. Pfanz, *Gettysburg-Culp's Hill and Cemetery Hill* [Chapel Hill, The University of North Carolina Press, 1993], 11
177. Philip M. Cole, *Civil War Artillery at Gettysburg*, 2nd ed. [Orrtanna, Colecraft Industries, 2006], 181
178. *Civil War Command and Strategy*, 35
179. *OR*, Vol. 34, Part 1, 19
180. Gen. John B. Gordon, *Reminiscences of the Civil War* [New York, Charles Scribner's Sons, 1903], 56
181. *Four Years Under Marse Robert*, 273-74
182. *Four Years Under Marse Robert*, 245-46
183. *OR*, Vol. 36, Part 1, Appendix G, 264-65
184. Rory Muir, *Tactics and the Experience of Battle in the Age of Napoleon* [New Haven, Yale university Press, 1998], 191-92
185. Grady McWhiney and Perry D. Jamieson, *Attack and Die* [University, The University of Alabama Press, 1982], 15
186. *OR*, Vol. 27, Part 2, 299
187. Douglas Southall Freeman, *Lee's Lieutenants* [New York, Charles Scribner's Sons, 1944], xiii
188. Dr. Ernest Butner, *The Art of War (Machiavelli, Vauban, and Frederick) Civil War Implications of Tactics* [www.civilwarhome.com/artofwar.htm]
189. *Four Years Under Marse Robert*, 361
190. *Personal Recollections of the Civil War*, 150
191. *OR*, Vol. 27, Part 3, 78-79
192. U.S. Army Military Museum, West Point, N.Y., Small Arms display
193. James Barnett, *Forty For the Union: Civil War Generals Buried in Spring Grove Cemetery*
194. *Understanding Fear's Effect on Unit Effectiveness*, 26
195. *Four Years Under Marse Robert*, 360
196. *Four Years Under Marse Robert*, 362
197. *Four Years Under Marse Robert*, 363-64
198. *Understanding Fear's Effect on Unit Effectiveness*, 27; *Personal Recollections of the Civil War*, 19
199. *Four Years Under Marse Robert*, 359
200. *Acts of War*, 25
201. *Battle Tactics of the Civil War*, 106
202. *The Passing of the Armies*, 96
203. *Understanding Fear's Effect on Unit Effectiveness*, 24, 26
204. *Acts of War*, 38, 40
205. *Acts of War*, 38, 40
206. *Understanding Fear's Effect on Unit Effectiveness*, 24, 26
207. *Attack and Die*, 44, 82

208. *The Union Soldier in Battle*, 114-15
209. *Pickett's Charge*, 90-91
210. *Acts of War*, 25, 158-59, *The Union Soldier in Battle*, 110
211. *OR*, Vol. 18, 895
212. *OR*, Vol. 2, 265
213. *Acts of War*, 138-39; *Photographic History f the Civil War: Forts and Artillery*, Vol. 3, 74
214. *OR*, Vol. 27, Part 3, 415
215. *Photographic History of the Civil War-Soldiers Life and Secret Service*, 166
216. *The Gettysburg Papers*, Vol. 1, 340
217. *Photographic History of the Civil War-Soldiers Life and Secret Service*, 168
218. *Gettysburg-Culp's Hill and Cemetery Hill*, 20
219. *Personal Recollections of the Civil War*, 132
220. *Photographic History of the Civil War-Soldiers Life and Secret Service*, 168, 170, 172
221. *The Gettysburg Papers*, Vol. 1, 340-42
222. Lt. Col. James Arthur Lyon Freemantle, Walter Lord, ed., *The Freemantle Diary* [Boston, Little, Brown and Company, 1954], 202-03
223. *The Twentieth Maine*, 115
224. *Photographic History of the Civil War-Soldiers Life and Secret Service*, 172, 174
225. *Four Years Under Marse Robert*, 330-331
226. *Photographic History f the Civil War: Forts and Artillery*, Vol. 3, 74
227. *Battle Tactics of the Civil War*, 111-12
228. *OR*, Vol. 10, Part 2, 326
229. *Photographic History of the Civil War-Soldiers Life and Secret Service*, 162
230. *Photographic History of the Civil War-Soldiers Life and Secret Service*, 174
231. *Tactics and the Experience of Battle in the Age of Napoleon*, 212
232. *OR*, Vol. 10, Part 1, 366
233. *The Union Soldier in Battle*, 110
234. *Understanding Fear's Effect on Unit Effectiveness*, 23
235. *OR*, Vol. 10, Part 1, 856
236. U. S. Government, *Report of the Joint Committee on the Conduct of the War, at the second session, Thirty-eighth Congress*, Vol. 2 [Kraus Reprint Co., 1977], 443
237. *Battle Tactics of the Civil War*, 62,108,112-13; *Pickett's Charge*, 167; *BP*, Vol. 3, 1744
238. *OR*, Vol. 9, 54
239. *Tactics and the Experience of Battle in the Age of Napoleon*, 212-14
240. *Psychological and Psychosocial Consequences of Combat and Deployment*

with Special Emphasis on the Gulf War, Chapter 3

241. *OR*, Vol. 11, Part 2, 629
242. *The Eleventh Corps Artillery at Gettysburg*, 38
243. *War as I Knew it*, 322
244. *OR*, Vol. 27, part 1, 689 [There is confusion as to which battery is involved in this incident. Maj. Osborn, 11th corps artillery brigade commander, claimed it was Norton's Battery H, First Ohio Light Artillery that left the field. His account was most likely connected with McCartney's account of Edgell's First New Hampshire leaving ammunition on the ground. Edgell relieved Norton in the same position.]
245. *OR*, Vol. 10, Part 2, 326
246. *OR*, Vol. 20, Part 1, 761
247. *OR*, Vol. 20, Part 1, 652
248. *OR*, Vol. 27, Part 3, 620-21
249. *Gettysburg: A Meditation on War and Values*, 239-40
250. *Gettysburg: A Meditation on War and Values*, 239-40
251. *BP*, Vol. 3, 1411
252. *OR*, Vol. 27, Part 2, 386
253. *OR*, Vol. 27, Part 1, 451
254. *Understanding Fear's Effect on Unit Effectiveness*, 23
255. *Understanding Fear's Effect on Unit Effectiveness*, 26
256. *Four Years Under Marse Robert*, 105-06
257. *Wartime-Understanding and Behavior in the Second World War*, 274
258. *The Eleventh Corps Artillery at Gettysburg*, 36
259. *The Eleventh Corps Artillery at Gettysburg*, 38
260. *Four Years Under Marse Robert*, 116
261. *Attack and Die*, 124
262. *Photographic History f the Civil War: Forts and Artillery*, Vol. 3, 74
263. *Tactics and the Experience of Battle in the Age of Napoleon*, 85
264. *Photographic History of the Civil War-Soldiers Life and Secret Service*, 174. David G. Martin, *Gettysburg, July 1* [Conshohocken, Combined Books, Inc., 1995], 359
265. Donald L. Smith, *The Twenty-Fourth Michigan* [Harrisburg, The Stackpole Co., 1962], 64; Edwin B. Coddington, *The Gettysburg Campaign, a Study in Command* [New York, Charles Scribner's Sons, 1968], 508
266. *OR*, Vol. 38, Part 3, 213
267. *OR*, Vol. 27, Part 1, 567
268. *The Union Soldier in Battle*, 112
269. *Human Interest Stories of the Gettysburg Campaign*, 64
270. *Human Interest Stories of the Gettysburg Campaign*, 60-61
271. *Human Interest Stories of the Gettysburg Campaign*, 95
272. *Four Years Under Marse Robert*, 220-21
273. *OR*, Series 3, Vol. 5, 285
274. *OR*, Vol. 11, Part 1, 458-59

275. *OR*, Vol. 30, Part 2 , 704
276. *OR*, Series 2, Vol. 5, **688**
277. Alexander Hunter, "A High Private's Sketch of Sharpsburg," *SHSP*, Vol. 32, 15-16
278. *Acts of War, 29*
279. Col. Charles S. Wainright, *Diary of a Battle*[Gettysburg, PA, Stan Clark Military Books, 1962], 237; *Gettysburg, July 1*, 180, 473-74
280. *OR*, Vol. 4, 249
281. *OR*, Vol. 22, Part 1 , 240
282. *Human Interest Stories of the Gettysburg Campaign*, 20-21
283. *OR*, Vol. 27, Part 3, 398
284. *OR*, Vol. 11, Part 2, 831
285. *OR*, Vol. 34, Part 1, 986
286. http://oha.alexandriava.gov/fortward/special-sections/mascots/; http://www.floridareenactorsonline.com/mascots.htm
287. *Four Years Under Marse Robert*, 234
288. *OR*, Vol. 27, Part 1, 883
289. *Four Years Under Marse Robert*, 235
290. *Human Interest Stories of the Gettysburg Campaign,* 76
291. *Human Interest Stories of the Gettysburg Campaign,* 61
292. *Human Interest Stories of the Gettysburg Campaign,* 62
293. *Reminiscences of the Civil War*, 6
294. *Reminiscences of the Civil War*, 7
295. *Citizen Soldier*,485; *Acts of War*, 231; *The American Soldier: Combat and its Aftermath. Studies in Social Psychology in World War II,* Vol. 2, 83
296. *The Gettysburg Papers.*, Vol. 1, 346
297. *Four Years Under Marse Robert*, 330
298. *The Union Soldier in Battle* 28-29
299. *Acts of War*, 15
300. Johnson, Robert Underwood and Clarence Clough Buel, eds., *Battles and Leaders of the Civil War*, Vol. 3 [New York, Thomas Yoseloff, 1956], 431
301. *Embattled Courage*, 241
302. Capt. Robert G. Carter, Heavy Artillery Regt., *The Gettysburg Papers*, Vol. 2, 709-10
303. William R. Cox, "Major-General Stephen D. Ramseur: His Life And Character," *SHSP*, Vol. 18, 242
304. *Four Years Under Marse Robert*, 97
305. *Four Years Under Marse Robert*, 98
306. "Major-General Stephen D. Ramseur: His Life And Character," *SHSP*, Vol. 18, 249
307. *Photographic History of the Civil War-Soldiers Life and Secret Service,* 164, 168
308. George Cary Eggleston, *A Rebel's Recollections* [New York, Hurd and Houghton- Cambridge: The Riverside Press, 1875, Access courtesy of

University of North Carolina at Chapel Hill] 50-51, 239-40

309. *The Art of War (Machiavelli, Vauban, and Frederick)*
Civil War Implications of Tactics[www.civilwarhome.com/artofwar.htm]

310. *Peaches and Pound Cake*, 40

311. Alicia Chang, AP Science Writer, *Military Experiment Seeks to Predict PTSD* Gettysburg Times, December 22, 2009], C4

312. Walter Reed Army Institute of Research, U.S. Army Medical Research and Materiel Command;
https://www.battlemind.army.mil/.../10_leaders_tough_facts_about_comba t_brief.pdf

313. https://www.battlemind.army.mil/.../pre_deployment/pre_deployment_ battlemind_for_warriors.ppt

Bibliography

Alexander, Edward Porter, Fighting for the Confederacy [Chapel Hill, University of North Carolina Press, 1989]

Ambrose, Stephan E., Citizen Soldier [New York, Simon and Schuster, 1998]

Bleier, Rocky, "A Prayer Remembered" [American Legion Magazine, January 2010]

Butner, Ernest, The Art of War (Machiavelli, Vauban, and Frederick) Civil War Implications of Tactics [www.civilwarhome.com/artofwar.htm]

Bandy Freeland, and Bearss,eds., The Gettysburg Papers-Addresses on the War 1861-65, Vol. 2, [Dayton, Morningside Bookshop, 1978]

Chamberlain, Joshua, The Passing of the Armies [Gettysburg, Stan Clark Military Books, 1994]
Chang, Alicia, Military Experiment Seeks to Predict PTSD [Gettysburg Times, December 22, 2009]

Coddington, Edwin B., The Gettysburg Campaign, a Study in Command [New York, Charles Scribner's Sons, 1968]

Cole, Philip M., Civil War Artillery at Gettysburg, 2nd ed. [Orrtanna, Colecraft Industries, 2006]

Crum, Herb S., ed., The Eleventh Corps Artillery at Gettysburg: The Papers of Major Thomas Ward Osborn, Chief of Artillery [Hamilton, Edmonston Publishing, Inc., 1991]

Daddis, Gregory A., Maj., U.S. Army, "Understanding Fear's Effect on Unit Effectiveness" [Military Review, July -August 2004]

DeBecker, Gavin, The Gift of Fear [New York, Little, Brown and Company], 1997

Eggleston, George Cary, A Rebel's Recollections [New York, Hurd and Houghton, Cambridge: The Riverside Press, 1875]

Fox, William F., Lt. Col., U.S.V., Fox's Regimental Losses [Albany, Albany Publishing Company, 1889],Chapter VII

Freeman, Douglas Southall, Lee's Lieutenants [New York, Charles Scribner's Sons,

1944]

Freemantle, James Arthur Lyon, Lt. Col., Walter Lord, ed., The Freemantle Diary [Boston, Little, Brown and Company, 1954]

Fussell, Paul, Wartime -Understanding and Behavior in the Second World War [New York, Oxford University Press, 1989]

Gibbon, John, Brig. Gen., Personal Recollections of the Civil War [Dayton, Morningside Bookshop, 1988]

Gordon, John B., Reminiscences of the Civil War [New York, Charles Scribner's Sons, 1903]

Gramm, Kent, Gettysburg: A Meditation on War and Values [Indianapolis, Indiana University Press, 1994]

Griffith,Paddy, Battle Tactics of the Civil War [New Haven, Yale University Press, 1989]

Edward Hagerman, The American Civil War and the Origins of Modern Warfare [Indianapolis, Indiana University Press, 1988]

Harrison, David, Adrenaline and Self Defense-Friend or Foe [http://www.kidpowervancouver.org/Article-Adrenaline.html]

Hess, Earl J., The Union Soldier in Battle [Lawrence, University Press of Kansas, 1997]

Holmes, Richard, Acts of War [New York, The Free Press, 1986]

Hunter, Alexander, "A High Private's Sketch of Sharpsburg" Southern Historical Society Papers [hereinafter known as SHSP], Vol. 11

Johnson, Paul M., Every Man Has His Breaking Point: The Attitudes of American Infantrymen Towards Combat Fatigue in World War II [Eau Claire, Department of History, University of Wisconsin, Research Seminar, Professor Thomas Miller, Cooperating Professor: Earl Shoemaker, By Paul M. Johnson, November 28, 2006]

Johnson, Robert Underwood and Clarence Clough Buel, eds., Battles and Leaders of the Civil War, Vol. 3 [New York, Thomas Yoseloff, 1956]

Jones, Archer, Civil War Command and Strategy [New York, The Free Press, 1992]

Jones, J. Wm., [Reply to Mr. Cazenove G. Lee, of Washington, in the table, which was published originally in the Baltimore Sun.] [From the Times-Dispatch, January 8, 1905.], SHSP, Vol. 32

Ladd, David L. & Audrey J., eds., The Bachelder Papers—Gettysburg in Their Own

Words, 3 Vols: Vols. 1 & 2, 1994, Vol. 3, 1995 [Dayton: Morningside House, Inc.], Hereafter referred to as BP.

Lash, Gary G., "141st Pa. At Gettysburg" [Gettysburg Magazine #14], 98

Linderman, Gerald F., Embattled Courage [New York, The Free Press, 1989]

Marlowe, David H., Psychological and Psychosocial Consequences of Combat and Deployment with Special Emphasis on the Gulf War, Chapter 3 [Rand Corporation, 2000]

Martin, David G., Gettysburg, July 1 [Conshohocken, Combined Books, Inc., 1995]

Meade, George G., The Life and Letters of George Gordon Meade, Vol. 2 [New York, Charles Scribner's Sons, 1913]

McPherson, James, For Cause and Comrades [New York, Oxford University Press, 1997]

McWhiney, Grady, and Perry D. Jamieson, Attack and Die [University, The University of Alabama Press, 1982]

Mingus, Sr., Scott L., Human Interest Stories of the Gettysburg Campaign [Orrtanna, Colecraft Industries, 2006]

Mingus, Sr., Scott, Human Interest Stories of the Gettysburg Campaign, Vol. 2, [Orrtanna, Colecraft Industries, 2007]

Mishori, Ranit, "Can Stress Make You Sick?" [Parade Magazine, 10/25/09]

Muir, Rory, Tactics and the Experience of Battle in the Age of Napoleon [New Haven, Yale university Press, 1998]

Ondishko, Jr., Joseph J., "A View of Anxiety, Fear, and Panic" [Military Affairs, Vol. 36, No. 2 [Society for Military History, Apr., 1972]

Patton, Jr., George S., War as I knew it, [New York, Bantam Books, 1980]

Pfanz, Harry W., Gettysburg, The Second Day [Chapel Hill, The University of North Carolina Press, 1987]

Pfanz, Harry W., Gettysburg-Culp's Hill and Cemetery Hill [Chapel Hill, The University of North Carolina Press, 1993]

Poague, Lt. Col. W. T., "At Gettysburg," Photographic History of the Civil War: Forts and Artillery, Vol. 3, [Secaucus, The Blue and Grey Press, 1987]

Pullen, John J., The Twentieth Maine [Dayton, Morningside Books, 1980]

Redwood, Allen C., "The Confederate in the Field," Photographic History of the Civil

War—Soldiers Life and Secret Service, Vol. 4 [Secaucus, The Blue and Grey Press, 1987]

Sauers, Richard A., "Rarely Has More Skill, Vigor, or Wisdom Been Shown": George G. Meade on July 3 at Gettysburg, essay in Three days at Gettysburg, Gary Gallagher, ed. [Kent, Kent State University Press, 1999]

Scales, Robert H., Maj. Gen., ret., "A Battlefield Too Even" [American Legion Magazine, 12/2006 issue]

Scales, Robert H., Maj. Gen., ret., "Peaches and Pound Cake" [The American Legion Magazine, January 2010]

Smith, Donald L., The Twenty-Fourth Michigan [Harrisburg, The Stackpole Co., 1962]

Smith, L. A., 1st Lt., 136th N. Y. Infantry, The Gettysburg Papers. 2 Vols. [Morningside Bookshop, 1978]

Southern Historical Society Papers, hereinafter referred to as SHSP, [Richmond, Va., February-March, 1883]

Starr, Stephen Z., The Union Cavalry in the Civil War, Vol. 1[Baton Rouge, Louisiana State University, 1979]

Stewart, George R., Pickett's Charge [Greenwich, Fawcett Publications, 1963]

Stiles, Robert, Maj. of Artillery in the Army of Northern Virginia, Four Years Under Marse Robert [New York and Washington, The Neale Publishing Company, 1904, third edition]

Stouffer, Samuel A., et al. The American Soldier: Combat and its Aftermath. Studies in Social Psychology in World War II, Vol. 2 [Princeton, NJ, Princeton University Press, 1949]

Swinton, William, Campaigns of the Army of the Potomac [Secaucus, The Blue and Grey Press, 1988]

Talbott, John, "Combat Trauma in the American Civil War" [History Today, Vol. 46, March, 1996]

Tzu, Sun, James Clavell, ed., The Art of War [Delacorte Press, New York, 1983]

U.S. War Department, The War of the Rebellion: A Compilation of the Official Records of the Union and Confederate Armies, 70 vols. In 128 parts, Hereinafter referred to as "OR, Vol.__, Part__, __." Unless noted, all references are from Series 1.

U. S. Government, *Report of the Joint Committee on the Conduct of the War, at the second session, Thirty-eighth Congress*, Vol. 2 [Kraus Reprint Co., 1977]

Wainright, Charles S., Diary of a Battle[Gettysburg, Stan Clark Military Books, 1962]

Watson,William, Life in the Confederate Army [New York, Scribner and Welford, 1983]

Webster's New Collegiate Dictionary [Springfield, G. & C. Merriam Company, 1973]

Weigley, Russell F., A Great Civil War [Indianapolis, Indiana University Press, 2000]

Digital Sources

http://www.battlemind.army.mil
http://www.civilwarhome.com/desertion2.htm
http://www.clausewitz.com/CWZHOME/On_War/BK1ch07.html
http://www.heartquotes.net/fear.html
http://www.kidpowervancouver.org/Article-Adrenaline.html
http://en.wikipedia.org/wiki/

Illustration Sources

Alfred R. Waud, Civil War Artist, Frederick E. Ray [New York, The Viking Press, 1974]

Battles and Leaders of the Civil War, Volumes 1-4 [New York, Thomas Yoseloff, Inc., 1956]

Battles and Leaders of the Civil War, Peter Cozzens, ed., Volume 5 [Chicago, University of Illinois Press, 2002]

The Civil War: The Artists' Record, Hermann Warner Williams, Jr., [Boston, Beacon Press, 1961]

Civil War in Pictures, Fletcher Pratt [Garden City, Garden City Books, 1955]

Harper's New Monthly Magazine, Volume 72 [New York, Harper Brothers, Publishers, 1886]

Harper's New Monthly Magazine, Volume 58 [New York, Harper Brothers, Publishers, 1879

Leslie's Illustrated Civil War [Jackson, University Press of Mississippi, 1992]

Library of Congress

Index

ABOUT THE AUTHOR

Philip M. Cole was born and raised in Gettysburg, Pennsylvania. As a youth, the battlefield was a place to ride bikes, take hikes, play in the rocks, and camp. Such intimate contact with the surroundings eventually grew into a lifelong interest in the historic events connected with his childhood "playground".

He is one of ten children. The family has a history of military tradition – he is one of seven of nine sons who volunteered, serving as a Russian linguist in the U. S. Navy. In the Civil War, his ancestors were members of the 76th Pennsylvania Infantry, the Keystone Zouaves, and involved in such battles as Fort Wagner and Cold Harbor.

The family is also connected with the battle of Gettysburg and battlefield monumentation. His great, great grandfather, Nicholas Codori, owned the farm that Pickett's division advanced across on July 3rd. A great, great uncle, Nicholas' brother George, was one of the handful of civilians taken back with Lee's army to spend a lengthy stay in a North Carolina prisoner of war camp.

Another uncle, Paul Roy, was Executive Secretary for the planning of the 75th battle anniversary and dedication of the Eternal Peace Light memorial. After five years, his persistent efforts finally convinced the veterans' leadership from both sides to have one last meeting on the old battleground. Philip's grandmother's horse, Dolly, was used as a model for the 1st Massachusetts Cavalry monument [near Gen. Sedwick's equestrian statue].

After receiving a Bachelor of Science degree in accounting from Pennsylvania State University, Philip was a regional control manager for an international corporation, founded a marketing company, and, eventually, a book publishing firm.

He has two daughters, lives near Gettysburg with his spouse, Diane, works as a Licensed Battlefield Guide at Gettysburg National Military Park, and is the author of two other books, *Civil War Artillery at Gettysburg* and *Command and Communication Frictions in the Gettysburg Campaign*.

Other Books by Colecraft:

Civil War Artillery at Gettysburg by Philip M. Cole

**Command and Communication Frictions
in the Gettysburg Campaign** by Philip M. Cole

Human Interest Stories of the Gettysburg Campaign
by Scott L. Mingus, Sr.

Human Interest Stories of the Gettysburg Campaign - Vol.2
by Scott L. Mingus, Sr.

Human Interest Stories from Antietam
by Scott L. Mingus, Sr.

A Concise Guide to the Artillery at Gettysburg
by Gregory A. Coco

Remarkable Stories of the Lincoln Assassination
by Michael Kanazawich

**A Strong and Sudden Onslaught
The Cavalry Action at Hanover, Pennsylvania**
by John T. Krepps

The Campaign and Battle of Gettysburg
by Col. G. J. Fiebeger

For Ordering Information:

Visit us at colecraftbooks.com or
e-mail us at: colecraftbooks@embarqmail.com

Wholesale orders may be placed with our distributing partner, Ingrams

CPSIA information can be obtained at www.ICGtesting.com
Printed in the USA
BVOW080248121011

273426BV00005B/1/P

9 780977 712595